THE BOOK OF
MURDER AND SCIENCE
VOL III

From the first fingerprint evidence in a murder trial in 1905 to recent advances in 'genetic fingerprinting', the techniques of forensic science have helped police to solve some of the most shocking crimes in history. Journalist and author Roger Wilkes has brought together a fascinating collection of forensic detective work, with cases from as early as 1752, to our own times. These trials, mostly successful but sometimes dangerously flawed, give a remarkable insight into the development and huge potential of science-based detection.

Edited By
ROGER WILKES

◆

THE BOOK OF
MURDER AND
SCIENCE
Volume III

Complete and Unabridged

ULVERSCROFT
Leicester

First published in Great Britain in 2000 by
Robinson
London

First Large Print Edition
published 2003
by arrangement with
Constable & Robinson Limited
London

British Library CIP Data

Wilkes, Roger, *1948* –
   The book of murder and science, Vol III edited by
Roger Wilkes.—Large print ed.—
Ulverscroft large print series: non-fiction
1. Forensic sciences 2. Murder—Investigation
3. Large type books
I. Wilkes, Roger, *1948* – II. Murder and science
614.1

   ISBN 0–7089–4799–9

Published by
F. A. Thorpe (Publishing)
Anstey, Leicestershire
Set by Words & Graphics Ltd.
Anstey, Leicestershire
Printed and bound in Great Britain by
T. J. International Ltd., Padstow, Cornwall

This book is printed on acid-free paper

CONTENTS

A WELSH MUMMY
(Sarah Jane Harvey, 1960)
Robert Jackson 1

A RAY OF SUNLIGHT UNMASKS A KILLER
(William Henry Podmore, 1930)
Tom Tullett 31

THE POISONER
(Kenneth Barlow, 1957)
Percy Hoskins.....................................54

THE JEKYLL AND HYDE OF NEW YORK
(Dr Arthur Waite, 1916)
John Laurence 67

THE TALKING SKULL
(Harry Dobkin, 1942)
Nigel Morland.....................................94

THE JIGSAW MURDER CASE
(Dr Buck Ruxton, 1935)
Jonathan Goodman.....................................125

A CASE OF 'HIDEOUS FEROCITY'
(Peter Griffiths, 1948)
Norman Lucas......................154

DR PARKMAN TAKES A WALK
(Professor John Webster, 1849)
Cleveland Amory......................176

THE MURDERER WHO GOT AWAY
WITH IT
(John Donald Merrett, 1926)
Macdonald Hastings......................211

PICTURE A MURDERER
(Edwin Bush, 1961)
Richard Jackson......................238

THE BITER BIT
(Gordon Hay, 1968)
George Saunders......................256

A WELSH MUMMY

(Sarah Jane Harvey, UK 1960)

Robert Jackson

The best-known case in Britain involving mummified remains is that of Mrs Sarah Harvey, tried for the murder of her lodger, Mrs Frances Knight, but acquitted. Mrs Knight's doubled-up body, shrouded in the mouldering remnants of her nightdress and dressing gown, was discovered in a locked cupboard at Mrs Harvey's house in Rhyl, North Wales, in 1960. Mrs Harvey said that she'd put Mrs Knight there after finding her dead in her room in April 1940. The skin was shrunken and leathery, and the corpse had been mummified by the natural process of warm, dry air rising and circulating in the cupboard, slowly drying out the body tissues. But suspicion arose during a post-mortem examination, prompted by a groove on the neck associated with the disintegrating vestige of a knotted stocking. The pathologist concluded that Mrs Knight had been strangled, and Mrs Harvey was charged with

1

murder. She denied the charge, and it was not supported by the physical evidence. Neither the hyoid bone nor thyroid cartilage was fractured, as would be expected in a case of strangulation. Cleared of murder, Mrs Harvey was nevertheless convicted of fraud, because for twenty years she had drawn a special pension to which her dead lodger had been entitled. Robert Jackson (1911–77), a Yorkshireman, was a journalist who worked as a foreign and war correspondent before turning to authorship with a series of biographies of twentieth century legal luminaries including the former Lord Chief Justice, Lord Hewart. Surprisingly, perhaps, he was also editor of Gardening Illustrated.

Of all the people who took part in the trial in October, 1960, of Mrs Sarah Jane Harvey, a sixty-five-year-old Rhyl, North Wales, landlady for murder, the most unremarkable was the woman in the dock.

The Solicitor-General, Sir Jocelyn Simon, QC, who prosecuted, was to become President of the Probate, Divorce and Admiralty Division of the High Court. Mr Elwyn Jones, QC his chief assistant, was picked by the Labour Prime Minister in 1964 to be Attorney-General. Professor Sir Sydney Smith, called the 'patriarch' of all forensic

2

experts, and Dr (later Professor) Francis E. Camps, one of the leading Home Office pathologists for a quarter of a century, attended to give advice to the defence on matters about which not more than a dozen men in the world could have spoken with authority. Sir Francis Walshe, the great neurological specialist was present, as was Lord Cohen of Birkenhead, the famous physician. Dr Edward Gerald Evans, Home Office pathologist for North Wales and West Midlands, was the chief prosecution witness and although the defence experts disagreed with his conclusions, they openly expressed admiration for his work. Not the least remarkable man in court was the defence counsel, Mr Andrew Rankin, a rugged figure, an expert in both Scottish and English law and a triple Blue (hockey, swimming and water polo) of both Edinburgh and Cambridge universities who, at thirty-six, took on a formidable team of prosecutors.

Yet the frail, ailing, drab little woman in the court had done something which extraordinary and ordinary people could not think of without revulsion. For twenty years, she had kept the mummified body of Mrs Frances Alice Knight, her lodger, in a locked cupboard at the top of the bedroom stairs. She was suspected of murder, accused of it,

3

and acquitted. As her counsel said, she must have gone through hell, knowing the body was there and that, having put it there, she could not turn back. With her secret always in danger of exploding, she walked the streets of the holiday town of Rhyl and except for her few friends nobody gave her a second look.

The case of the Mummy in the Cupboard, as it came to be called, was followed by the public for a number of reasons. To begin with, mummies are not found in cupboards every day of the week in Britain. The trial when it was held at Ruthin, the little assize town in Denbighshire, came to an end immediately after exhaustive cross-examination of the Crown's two principal witnesses, but particularly of the pathologist, Dr Evans. The two defence crime doctors, Sir Sydney Smith and Dr Camps, were present throughout. They did not give evidence but the knowledge that they were there — and what they would say if they were called — had a profound effect. There was another fact which made the trial interesting, although it was not revealed at the time. Barristers in murder trials have been experts on guns, poisons and other technical matters but the defence counsel, Mr Rankin, had an unusual qualification. For two years, he had studied medicine at Edinburgh University under one of his own forensic experts, Sir Sydney Smith.

To a large extent, Mrs Sarah Jane Harvey was responsible for her own predicament. Mrs Knight, the estranged wife of a Rhyl dentist who had gone in 1936 to live in Hove, Sussex, took a 30s. a week bed-sitting room in Mrs Harvey's house in West Kinmel Street early in 1940. The exact date she went there was not certain but a policeman handed her personally on February 27, 1940, the magistrates' order awarding her £2 a week for maintenance at the time she was living in another Rhyl boarding house. Mrs Knight found difficulty in walking from what was first thought to be rheumatism but turned out later to be disseminated sclerosis, a deadly crippling disease. She managed to get to the magistrates' office to collect the first payment. The second payment was made to Mrs Harvey, who showed the clerk's experienced assistant, Mr Albert Reveley, a chit signed by Mrs Knight authorizing her to collect the money. She continued to do so until she went into hospital herself with suspected cancer in April, 1960.

The death of Mrs Knight came to light in an unusual way, too. While Mrs Harvey was undergoing treatment in hospital her son Leslie, a taxi driver, decided to do his mother a good turn. Mrs Harvey had no lodger but as she had given Leslie the key he began to redecorate the house. Leslie had lived in the house all his life until two years after he married, when he found a place of his own. It had often puzzled him why his mother had never allowed the cupboard built on to the wall at the top of the stairs to be opened but he accepted her story that it contained various articles belonging to a former lodger who one day would want them back. Leslie Harvey decided to make a good job of decorating the top landing and deal with the cupboard inside and out. He forced one of the doors with a screwdriver and peered through the dark, musty-smelling cobwebby interior with the aid of a torch. It was a severe shock when he saw what seemed to be a human foot. His wife was downstairs and he hurried her off to her father's house. The two men returned together to the house and immediately they had made certain that what was inside the cupboard was a body, they sensibly hurried to the police station for help.

A local doctor was called but realized that the task of examining a mummified body would have to be undertaken by a highly-skilled pathologist and within a few hours Dr Evans and Dr Alan Clift, a biologist from the Home Office Forensic Laboratory at Preston, had begun to unravel the mystery of the mummy in the cupboard.

Bodies do not become mummies in a day or two in cold, damp climates and the obvious person to question first was Mrs Harvey, who had lived in the house for over forty years. Mrs Harvey was naturally shocked to hear of the mummy in the cupboard. She was a respectable as well as a sick woman and the only blemish on her character was a conviction for the theft of £10 in 1942.

Her first reaction when the police called to see her was to feign surprise and say she knew nothing about the mummy. No doubt with thoughts of her own illness uppermost in her mind she forgot any prepared story — if in the course of twenty years living with the mummy she had ever had one clearly mapped out.

But Mrs Harvey was sharp and knew her way about. She must have realized quickly that the police would not shrug off the finding of the mummy as one of those inexplicable things that happen. They had already questioned Leslie about the lodgers he remembered and the name of Mrs Knight, a lodger in his boyhood days, had cropped up. Yes, Mrs Harvey told the police, she knew Mrs Knight, a crippled lady, who had lived with her until the end of the war. She now lived in Penymaes, Llandudno, with a Mrs Collins. Mrs Harvey said she was sure of that because every week, she still collected £2 due to Mrs Knight under a maintenance order and posted it on, either in cash or as a postal order.

The police made a note to look up Mrs Knight in Penymaes and asked her about other lodgers who might know something about the mummy in the cupboard. Mrs Harvey took her time to answer but eventually she said she did remember a couple, named White or Wright. They had come to Rhyl at the time the bombing started in the South of England. Mrs Harvey said they wanted to store 'stuff and foodstuff' and she had let them use the landing cupboard. They had the key and went off with it about the end of the war. For two Christmases in succession she had had cards from the couple but they never returned to collect whatever it was they had left in the cupboard.

Mrs Harvey had furnished streets, places and names so that the police could trace Mrs Knight but they were unsuccessful. Mrs Harvey was being discharged from hospital temporarily but instead of going home she went, by invitation, to the police station.

She now decided that the time for fencing

was over. The police had held her on a charge of obtaining one of Mrs Knight's weekly instalments of £2 by false pretences and in the cells she began to unburden herself. 'Mrs Knight is in the cupboard,' she informed Chief Inspector H. I. Williams. 'I will tell you what happened. She died in the bedroom and I put her in the cupboard.'

Bit by bit, the secret she had bottled up for twenty years came out. She said that soon after coming to lodge with her, Mrs Knight became very frail and weak and developed great pains in her knees. Four or five weeks after she arrived, Mrs Harvey was getting ready for bed in the back bedroom, when she heard Mrs Knight screaming in her own bedroom. 'I went into the bedroom and saw her lying on the floor in her nightdress and coat. I asked her what had happened and she said 'I am in an awful lot of pain and would rather be dead'.'

Mrs Harvey said she tried to pick her distressed lodger up but could not manage it. She dressed herself and went downstairs to make tea but when she returned, Mrs Knight was still lying on the floor and was dead. 'I was on my own in the house and was scared stiff, so I pulled her along the landing and put her into the empty cupboard,' she said. 'I put fly-papers in the cupboard and then locked it.

I didn't tell anyone she had died — but I kept trying to keep things covered up. I have gone through hell ever since. I have told you everything now and that is the truth.'

The Rhyl detectives now had plenty of clues to follow up — apart from what the work of the pathologists would yield — since it was clear that Mrs Harvey's story would have to undergo the most stringent tests. Sudden death in a quiet house to a woman on her own can be a frightening experience but the question in the minds of the police and lawyers was simple: which was the more frightening thing to do — run into the house of a friendly neighbour and get help, or drag a freshly-dead body out on the landing, somehow — remembering that Mrs Harvey had said she could not lift Mrs Knight from the floor into bed — get her into the cupboard and wedge a bedspread between her thighs to prevent pollution.

A first thought was that Mrs Harvey, seeing Mrs Knight dead on the floor, suddenly realized that if only she could conceal the body she would in effect have inherited a pension of £2 a week. The prosecution at her trial went further and suggested that Mrs Harvey had done more than that — she had actually strangled Mrs Knight herself with a stocking so that she could continue to draw the money. The court did not accept the view but over the years, Mrs Harvey *did* collect £2,098 paid over by Mr Knight from Hove.

Mrs Harvey had also taken good care to see that the arrangement was not disturbed. The clerks in the magistrates' office showed an interest in their 'clients' and often asked how Mrs Knight, whom they never saw, was getting on. Mrs Harvey's replies varied week by week, from 'about the same' to 'a little better' or 'not too good'. Occasionally at Christmas, Mrs Harvey negotiated for the money to be paid in advance and when it did not turn up, the clerks were surprised to hear that the invalid would be in a 'bloody bad temper' or would 'play hell' in consequence.

When the trial took place, Mr Reveley, one of the senior clerks, was questioned closely by Mr Rankin about the office system which had allowed Mrs Harvey to draw the money for so long. Mrs Harvey's signed authority could not be found in the files but Mr Reveley remembered that she had handed it over. It had never occurred to him to doubt her honesty. 'I have known her forty or forty-five years and have always found her perfectly straightforward,' he said.

In 1949, the dead woman in the cupboard

must have been very much on Mrs Harvey's conscience because she sold a black trunk which had belonged to Mrs Knight and had her initials stamped on it. She remarked to the buyer that she did not think Mrs Knight would ever come back for it.

Mrs Harvey had undoubtedly taken trouble to keep inquisitive lodgers away from the cupboard. A miner who lodged with Mrs Harvey when he worked at a Rhyl colliery was traced to Newark. He said he and his wife were 'a bit nosey' when they lived in the house for periods in 1950 and 1951 and had tried to open the cupboard. He lost interest in it when Mrs Harvey told him that it contained her best linen.

But the most significant discovery which the police thought cast great doubt on Mrs Harvey's story was a fly-paper found hanging from the roof of the cupboard. Mrs Harvey said that from the day Mrs Knight was put in the cupboard in the early spring of 1940, the door had remained locked. This could not have been true. The fly-paper bore a code number and the name of the manufacturer at Derby. That particular batch of fly-papers, the manager said, could not have been on sale before the early spring of 1942 — a whole year after Mrs Knight's death.

Some of these matters could be drowned or

at least obscured by the vigorous cross-examination to which Mr Rankin subjected every witness. But in the end, the case against Mrs Harvey depended on the evidence given — or to be given — by the doctors who had treated Mrs Knight in life and those who had known her as what Dr Camps called 'a shell of dried skin and bones'.

Mrs Harvey, even twenty years before her trial, had not been particularly robust and part of the Crown case was that she was able to kill because Mrs Knight was 'vulnerable'. 'You may think that the fact that Mrs Knight was a cripple is significant in considering whether she would not be an easy victim of attack,' said the Solicitor-General, in opening the case.

Mrs Knight's friend, Mrs Phyllis Rogers, partially upset the idea that Mrs Knight was always miserable, complaining, and by inference, almost helpless. She produced a holiday snapshot which showed Mrs Knight looking quite happy, though admittedly she walked with a stick. 'She was cheerful with a keen sense of humour,' said Mrs Rogers. 'She never complained of pain.' Mrs Rogers maintained that though her condition was slowly deteriorating, Mrs Knight was chiefly worried because she was losing her sense of balance.

Mrs Rogers had taken Mrs Knight to Liverpool to see the famous consultant physician, Lord Cohen of Birkenhead, who had diagnosed disseminated sclerosis but anticipated that there would be some improvement in her condition. Mrs Knight's medical records showed that she was slightly overweight and there was nothing in them to suggest that she would die from natural causes within a short period.

But Sir Francis Walshe, the neurologist, advised the defence on a point in Mrs Harvey's favour. Her counsel took it up with Lord Cohen, who agreed that Mrs Knight had been suffering from a kidney infection which, in an acute form, might lead to death. He said anyone predisposed to the infection might fall dangerously ill suddenly and die within a fortnight. So, one of the most distinguished physicians went on the court record with the view that it was *possible* for Mrs Harvey's account of Mrs Knight's death to be correct.

The case reached the beginning of its crucial stage when crime doctor Gerald Evans stepped into the witness box to tell of the discovery and detailed examination of the mummy. There is a great deal of *camaraderie* among crime doctors, though they often speak in slighting terms of each other's work when talking privately. But there is no tendency for them to hang together and in most cases the cross-examination of counsel, usually based on the opinions of other crime doctors, are as a rule searching and prolonged. In the mummy case, Dr Evans was to be put to the fiercest test.

The mummy, it turned out, was not a 'true' mummy, though the difference between 'true' and 'false' could be appreciated only by crime doctors. Mummification was drying until the moisture was removed from the tissues, said Dr Evans. The passage of a current of dry air over the body, day and night, led to mummification and the preservation of the features and contours of the body. It was well known in Egypt.

In the case of the Rhyl mummy, mummification might have occurred because of a freak of chance. For many weeks and months, warm, dry air had circulated up the stairs into the landing and cupboard where the body lay. A small trap door above the cupboard may have helped the draughts. Dr Camps said later that the explanation was over-simplified but he admitted that it seemed to satisfy the jury. Gruesome photographs of the body were handed up to Mr Justice Davies, who seemed to approve of them on the principle that one picture is worth a thousand words.

It had been late at night when Dr Evans climbed the carpeted stairs of Mrs Harvey's house and in the light of police torches began to make clinical observations on the contents of the cupboard. Laymen in the old courthouse at Ruthin listened in a kind of awed wonder.

The sight he saw was not pretty — the fly-paper saturated with flies, the thick cobwebs on the walls to which dead spiders clung in grotesque masses, and the object on the floor that had been a woman. Here the lacey cobwebs were several inches deep. He could also make out the shape of a mound of mould and literally many hundreds of pupa cases from which maggots had emerged as flies. They told their own story of what had happened when the natural putrefaction of the body set in.

A foot was visible, brown and skinny, as Leslie Harvey had seen it. Moving closer into the smell of decay, Dr Evans gently began to brush aside the cobwebs, mould and dust. He uncovered what had been a human face with nostrils dilated and lips stretched and distorted. But immediately he had had to retreat on to the landing to cough out the dust that rose in clouds and choked him.

The greatest care was obviously necessary in recovering the mummy and Dr Evans examined the cupboard to see whether he could unscrew it to take it away. But the cupboard had been built on to the wall and it could not be done. So he began again to stir the dust as gently as possible and after a time he saw the outline of the mummy under a crumbling blue dressing gown and blanket. He had to remove two more types of material before the mummy was completely exposed — the bedspread, which had been packed between the legs, and a long-sleeved night-dress, the V-shaped neck of which could be traced.

The mummy under the touch of his fingers was rock hard — an absolute statue, Dr Evans said in court. It was lying on its back with the thighs bent backwards towards the abdomen and the legs bent or flexed at the knees. The left arm was extended down the side of the body and the right forearm, with a claw-like hand, lay across the chest. The whole of the skin from the neck to the feet was peppered with maggot holes.

Dr Evans's experience in removing the crumbling matter other than the body had made him apprehensive about what would happen when he attempted to take the mummy out of the cupboard but he need not have worried. Far from disintegrating, he could not budge the mummy. Finally, he saw only one solution. He would have to lever it from the cupboard floor. 'Get me a spade,' he said to the police.

In his own mortuary, Dr Evans made a detailed examination of the mummy before he put it in a bath containing a solution of glycerine to soften it. The mummy's head was turned to the right and when the dust had been brushed from the neck, he saw a distinct groove with a localized depression at the front. A great deal was to be heard at the trial about the groove. He tilted the mummy to see whether the groove ran all the way round the neck. It did, and what appeared to have caused the groove — a piece of tape-like material — fell away. A further piece of the same material was still embedded in the groove and when Dr Evans had eased it out he saw that it was part of a stocking. There was only a few inches of it altogether — the fragments were exhibited in a test-tube in court — but it contained an undoubted reef knot.

As Dr Evans said in court, the body was in a 'deplorable' condition but the post-mortem on the mummy, and later the examination of the skeleton, produced a very adequate build-up of the sort of person the mummy had been in life. She was a European woman between forty and sixty, nearly 5 ft, 4 ins, tall with shapely ears. She was married — her ring finger was grooved but — another minor mystery — the ring was not in the cupboard.

She could not have had children without a Caesarian operation. She was right-handed and dragged her left foot when she walked. In her early teens, she had had an illness which had been cured by medicine containing arsenic, lead or iron. All her teeth had been extracted but her dentures were missing. Many of the internal organs had been eaten away over the years but the crime doctors did not think she had been poisoned. They had even been able to find her blood group. They compared it with blood groups of Mrs Knight's close relatives and, if they had been called to give an opinion in court, would have said that Mrs Knight's group might well have been that of the mummy's.

The defence discussed the possibility of trying to prove that the mummy in the cupboard was not that of Mrs Knight, relying on a legal objection to Mrs Harvey's own admission. The idea was quickly abandoned and the line they were to take became apparent soon after the cross-examination of Dr Evans began.

Dr Evans had been taken through his evidence-in-chief by the Solicitor-General and had told the court how he had seen the groove around the neck and retrieved the piece of stocking, with the tightly tied reef knot. When he put the stocking on the postmortem bench, it remained in a curve and this suggested that at one time it had encircled the neck. 'If you tie a stocking tightly round a person and knot it and take the stocking off fairly soon after, you will get no depression. But if that stocking is left in contact with the skin over a period of time, then, especially after mummification starts, I think it is more than probable that an indentation would remain,' he said.

There had been a depression on the side of the thyroid cartilage and he had found a knot in the stocking, but not where the depression was. Dr Evans found the groove on the left side difficult to associate with a natural fold of the neck and there was nothing in the cupboard which would account for the external pressure.

'Are you able on medical grounds, excluding the fact that you found a stocking, to state what was the cause of death?' asked Sir Jocelyn. 'No,' was the reply, 'I am afraid I cannot do that to help the court.'

'So that within your province as an expert, there is nothing to indicate what had happened?' The answer was 'No'.

Mr Rankin, impressive and confident,

plunged into battle and Dr Evans told him that it was quite impossible to determine whether the stocking had been put round Mrs Knight's neck before or after death.

The judge intervened. 'That is your opinion now?' 'Yes.'

'In your opinion now, was there or was there not a ligature?' pursued the judge. 'Yes, there was a ligature.'

Dr Evans explained that if there was a collar round the neck of a dead man and the skin became swollen, there would be a groove.

Said Mr Rankin: 'Sir Sydney Smith and Dr Camps, whose experience is unrivalled, say that this was never a homicidal ligature.' 'I could well understand that,' came the wry answer.

'They say that what you saw on the neck was caused by postmortem changes in the body, there having been before death what I have described as a natural ligature round the neck,' said Mr Rankin. 'That is an opinion I cannot agree with,' answered Dr Evans.

'Could a groove made by a collar be mistaken for a homicidal groove?' 'Not by a forensic pathologist.'

Mr Rankin commented that, 'We will see what another forensic expert will say' and Dr Evans thereupon amplified his answer. 'If this body does not disrupt but goes on to a more drying process, I think this groove would disappear and the skin flatten out again.'

'You think it disappears but leaves a mark?' queried Mr Rankin. 'Yes.'

Mr Rankin's comment that, 'the difficulty you are labouring under is lack of experience of this kind of case' brought from Dr Evans the complaint: 'I think you are putting it rather hardly.'

It was, as Dr Evans had admitted, only the second case of a mummy he had dealt with but he had been in no way put out when Mr Rankin told him that every year Dr Camps, whose opinion differed from his on several aspects of the case, saw about four cases a year. 'Four mummies twenty years old?' exclaimed Dr Evans, incredulously. 'I am only sorry he has not written up his experiences.'

Mr Rankin justifiably made all the capital he could from the fact that the thyroid cartilage had been accidentally fractured by an ear, nose and throat specialist to whom it had been sent for an opinion on possible abnormalities — Dr Evans had made it clear that when he first saw the cartilage, it was not fractured — and also because the neck skin had been cut up into many pieces during Dr Evans's investigation. Why had this been done, asked Mr Rankin.

'I thought it was necessary so as to identify any haemorrhages under the skin. But I found none. Laboriously I went on,' said Dr Evans.

'You went on cutting it up into small pieces?' asked Mr Rankin. 'You were doing away with what is regarded as a very important piece from the neck. This very important exhibit, which contains what is said to be a tightly-tied knot, was sent by registered post to the forensic laboratory, and in the post things could happen?' 'I agree,' said Dr Evans.

Mr Rankin returned later to the question of the skin collar. 'My experts find it difficult to understand why in this case the skin collar does not show a groove running right round the neck.' said Mr Rankin. Retorted Dr Evans: 'Your experts — and I am sorry this has to be — have not seen the skin collar as a whole, but only a portion of it.'

There was whispering between counsel and the defence pathologists. 'I am informed by them that they saw a major part of the collar,' said Mr Rankin. 'Do you agree?' 'No.'

'If it had been preserved, there would have been some degree of certainty?' Countered Dr Evans: 'Your experts could have had a much better chance of seeing what I saw.'

'They have seen enough to be exceedingly

puzzled why it is that some of the skin shows no groove marks at all,' said Mr Rankin. 'Would you agree that it would be reasonable to conclude from that, that there was post-mortem change with swelling which caused the mark you saw on the neck at the post-mortem?'

Dr Evans would not agree. 'I would rather expect Sir Sydney Smith and Dr Camps to see the difficulty of this particular case, with glycerine as an additive,' he said. A few questions later, he did not conceal his exasperation. 'I am trying to be completely scientific and I am not prepared to be dogmatic, as apparently some are,' he said.

There was little wonder that after nearly twelve hours in the witness box, Dr Evans became annoyed at the tone of some of the questions, in spite of honeyed words about his fairness. 'You do twist things, don't you,' he exclaimed to Mr Rankin at one point. 'It's very difficult for me to put anything across.'

The ligature had been put round Mrs Knight's neck either by Mrs Knight herself or by someone else and the defence developed an ingenious theory that Mrs Knight was wearing the stocking as a cure for a cold. It was no more than an idea which, according to some observers, made the court murmur in surprise. No doubt. Perhaps the surprise was felt at the idea of the wife of a professional man believing in such an old-fashioned remedy, quite apart from the fact that there was no evidence whatever that Mrs Knight had had a cold.

Dr Evans had not excluded the possibility that Mrs Knight had died naturally for the simple reason that he had very little tissue to work on. He was asked whether she could have died from a heart attack, lung infection like lobar pneumonia, bladder, kidney, or other infection. The answer in each case was 'yes' because Dr Evans had already said that he did not know the cause of death. Why then, he was asked, was it suggested that Mrs Knight was strangled with a stocking? He replied that there were six reasons — the neck groove, the depression on the neck, the depression on the thyroid cartilage, the ligature itself, the tightness of the ligature and finally, the evidence as a whole.

After much sound, fury and wind, Dr Evans had conceded little at the end of his cross-examination and the only important point for the Solicitor-General to re-emphasize was how the distortion of the thyroid cartilage had occurred. 'Is there any question of it taking place as a result of dissection?' he asked.

'In my opinion, no, or I would readily say

so,' affirmed Dr Evans.

The case for the prosecution was concluded with the evidence given by Dr Alan Clift, the biologist who had gone to Rhyl on the night of the discovery of the mummy. The fragments of stocking round Mrs Knight's neck were not much to go on but he said they showed that originally the stocking had been stretched tightly round her neck. Not only had the stocking been stretched but the fragment was the typical shape of a ligature. He was emphatic that the stretching had not occurred by the natural process of the swelling of the neck. He was asked whether the stretching of the stocking was of a homicidal character and his reply was 'yes', with the surprise proviso that he could not rule out suicide.

Mr Rankin challenged the evidence of Dr Clift as vigorously as he had done that of Dr Evans. The late Lord Birkett in the Rouse case had confounded an engineering expert because he did not know the co-efficient of the expansion of brass and Mr Rankin attempted a similar manœuvre. He drew from Dr Clift an admission that he did not know how to distinguish between American, Egyptian and Indian cotton. Nevertheless Dr Clift answered firmly 'I do', when he was asked whether he considered himself an expert on fabrics. Dr Clift agreed that he could find no other evidence on the stocking breaking under tension except that of insect attack.

At this point, Mr Justice Davies interrupted counsel's cross-examination. 'The allegation here is that this stocking was used by the prisoner to strangle this woman. The vital question is 'Has it been unduly stretched?' That is the first question to my mind that should have been asked.'

Mr Rankin bowed to the judge and asked Dr Clift whether he would be interested to learn that the defence had been to the Manchester Chamber of Commerce Commercial Testing House and their conclusion was that the stocking had not been abnormally stretched. 'I don't agree,' said Dr Clift.

It was clear that not only did the crime doctors disagree about the conclusions to be drawn from the marks on the body but that the fabric experts on both sides would be diametrically opposed.

Mr Eric Jones, director of the Testing House, had carried out a number of tests at the request of Mrs Harvey's advisers on how much tension would have been required to strangle Mrs Knight with a stocking. His conclusion, stripped of its technical terms, was that there was no evidence that the stocking round the mummy's neck had been under any abnormal tension, although the experts would not go as far as to say that the stocking had never been under an abnormal stretching force.

Dr Clift, before his evidence was complete, had fainted in the witness box and while the court waited for him to recover counsel for both sides talked the case over informally outside. The weakness of the prosecution case had been exposed and the Solicitor-General took the decision not to pursue it further.

The Judge was informed in his private room and later, in open court, Sir Jocelyn said that after considering his duty, the state of the case and the evidence so far, it would not be right to invite the jury to find a verdict of guilty.

For once in the case, the experts — this time on law — agreed. 'There seemed to be manifold circumstances of suspicion in the case,' said Mr Justice Davies. 'But when one considers the evidence of Dr Evans, which was given with conspicuous skill, fairness and moderation, it comes to this: he cannot say whether the ligature was put on before or after death and he cannot say that the ligature caused death. If it cannot be proved that the stocking stretched, then the prosecution fails. Without saying any more; because we have not heard the defence evidence, it does appear that the prosecution are in no position to prove that the stocking was stretched.'

The money to defend Mrs Harvey had been raised privately and Mr Graham Roberts, the young defence solicitor — like Mr Rankin, engaged on his first murder case — said that the considerable sum of £3,000 had been spent. When the jury had found Mrs Harvey not guilty of murder, Mr Rankin applied for costs. 'I appreciate that it could be said that this lady left herself open to this kind of charge,' observed Mr Rankin. 'But whatever lies she may have told, or cold, cool, calculating woman she may have been, in the end the prosecution case came down to two witnesses, Dr Evans and Dr Clift.' The heavy costs incurred by the defence, he said, had been in respect of those witnesses.

The Solicitor-General rose to his feet to resist the application but the judge stopped him. 'I don't think I need trouble you, Mr Solicitor,' he said. 'No, Mr Rankin,' he added, dismissing the application.

Two token charges of fraud concerning Mr Knight's maintenance payments remained to be dealt with and Mr Justice Davies rejected Mr Rankin's suggestion that Mrs Harvey should be allowed to go free after her years of terrible strain. The judge said the medical evidence before him showed that Mrs Harvey was a very sick woman. But taking into account the frightful anxiety she had undergone, the fact that she had been on trial for murder and had been imprisoned for four months awaiting trial, it was still impossible to overlook the case. The sentence was fifteen months' imprisonment.

Sniffing smelling salts, supported by a nurse and a wardress, the inconspicuous figure of Mrs Harvey passed from the dock, without having said a word about her long and extraordinary ordeal. Nor were the comments of Mr Knight, the loser almost by chance of more than £2,000, ever made available.

A RAY OF SUNLIGHT UNMASKS A KILLER

(William Henry Podmore, UK 1930)

Tom Tullett

When the great pathologist Sir Bernard Spilsbury examined the hammer used to murder Vivian Messiter, he found a single hair adhering to the hammer head. It matched the hair from Messiter's eyebrows, proving that the hammer had indeed dealt the fatal blow. But Messiter's killer, William Podmore, was brought to book not by a single hair but a single piece of flimsy paper. It was, as one criminologist observed, a case of small clues and large inferences, which is why it remains of exceptional interest to the student of modern crime detection. Indentations were found on a page of a receipt book, produced by the pressure of the pencil through another sheet on which some figures and initials had been written. The initials — W. F. T. — were those of Podmore's alias, William F. Thomas. Photographs were taken of these tell-tale indentations using a strong light thrown on them from an oblique angle. This cast a shadow across the indentations, enabling the eye to read them quite clearly. Because this scrap of paper linked Podmore with his victim, and was a vital part of the evidence against him, the case is notable as a triumph for forensic photography. Tom Tullett (1915–91) was chief of the Daily Mirror's crime bureau and the only journalist to have been a member of the Criminal Investigation Department at Scotland Yard. With Douglas G. Browne, Tullett wrote the standard biography of Spilsbury in the early 1950s.

By the end of the 1920s, murder investigations had gained some sense of order, and the countrywide search for the killer of a man who had been dead for more than two months when his body was found shows how the use of technical aids and methods of record-keeping were paying off.

At 6.45 on the evening of 10 January 1929 a telegram from Mr McCormac, Chief Constable of Southampton, was received at Scotland Yard. It read: 'A case of murder has occurred here. A man has been found shot dead in a room the door of which was padlocked. The body was found today and has probably been in the room for some eight or nine weeks. Will you please send an officer down to investigate the matter.'

Detective Chief Inspector John Prothero was tall and commanding and his colleagues called him 'Gentleman John'. He was always immaculately dressed, and spoke in an accent thought then to be the mark of a university education. He wore spats and had his shirt cuffs showing, at that time a rich man's luxury. But he was not rich, nor had he been to university. He was a great detective, who decided he wanted to be better dressed than the rest of his colleagues. He never raised his voice, never appeared to be angry, but his quiet insistence got the facts he required.

Prothero took with him to Southampton Sergeant Hugh Young, a Scot from the Black Isle in Ross and Cromarty. Like others before him he was a country boy who rose to command the Squad, and the experience he gained on this particular case was a great stepping-stone in his distinguished career.

The detectives went first to the Southampton mortuary to see the body of the victim, Vivian Messiter. The local police surgeon said that the murder had taken place some weeks before, and Messiter had last been seen alive on 30 October 1928. The body was in a bad state of decomposition and the rats had been busy, so that the features of the dead man were unrecognizable.

Vivian Messiter had been found in a lock-up garage-cum-storeroom at 42 Grove Street, Southampton, where he carried on business as a local agent of the Wolf's Head Oil Company, whose head offices were in London. He had not been seen alive since he left his lodgings at 3 Carlton Road on the morning of 30 October. He was a quiet man of regular habits, and when he failed to return home as usual his landlord, Mr Parrott, an ex-policeman, informed the police he was missing.

An officer went to the garage, but on finding the place securely padlocked from the outside, concluded that wherever Messiter was, he was not in the garage.

Mr Parrott wrote to Messiter's employers, reporting his lodger's absence. They asked him to visit the garage and, by breaking a window and peering through the aperture with the help of a candle, he could see that Messiter's car was safe and that nothing appeared to be amiss. It was concluded that Messiter had simply walked out of his job and had, perhaps, returned to the United States, where he had spent many years of his life. The subsequent lack of interest in his whereabouts was one of the striking features of the case.

Messiter was a member of an old Somersetshire family, educated at a minor public school. As a young man he had gone to the States with his brother Edgar and together they started a horse-breeding ranch in New Mexico. When Edgar drifted into mining operations in Colorado, Vivian went into business in Denver. Later he went to New York City, where the new subway railroad under the Hudson River was in course of construction. Such was his energy and ability to handle men that he rose from a subordinate position to the office of Chief Engineering Constructor. He became so well-known in this capacity that engineers from England were invited to meet him.

At the outbreak of the First World War he was wealthy and generally prosperous. He came home and enlisted, was commissioned in the Northumberland Fusiliers and went to fight in France. He was shot through both thighs and he remained slightly lame for the rest of his life. In 1928 he was fifty-seven, a reserved, solitary man, divorced from his wife, and he returned to England that year from another long absence in the United States and Mexico. Yet he had relatives in this country, and he had a job, and the fact that he was lost to sight and knowledge for more than two months without any serious efforts being made to discover what had become of him throws a curious light on the casual attitude of his friends and family and of the firm which not only employed him, but had recently made him a director.

Messiter's job was that of local agent for the Wolf's Head Oil Company and the garage in Grove Street was his headquarters. It was not until 10 January that this firm sent a Mr Passmore to take over the agency. With a friend Passmore gained access to the outer yard of the garage via the roof of the Royal Exchange public house next door. The garage was a long, narrow building with white-washed walls. Along the right-hand side was a double row of oil drums upon which boxes were piled. More boxes were stacked at the end, and in a recess was the body of Messiter lying face upwards.

After moving the body to the mortuary local police searched the garage. On the back seat of Messiter's car they found a duplicate order book and a memorandum book, from both of which a number of pages had been torn out. On one page of the memorandum book was a receipt signed by a Mr H. H. Galton for 2s 6d commission on the sale of five gallons of oil, dated 30 October, the last day Messiter was seen alive. The next page had been torn out, but on the following page were the words: 'Cromer & Bartlett, 25 Bold Street, 5 gallons heavy'. In the duplicate order book there was no writing of any kind, but, tucked away at the end of it, were two sheets of carbon paper on which could be just seen some names and addresses. The first was 'Cromer & Bartlett' of Bold Street, Southampton. Then there was a note, 'Sold to Ben Baskerfield, Clayton Farm, Bentley Road, near Winchester' and a third entry, 'Ben Jervis, Crescent Bassett, 5 gallons number 8 at 5s 6d'.

When the Yard men went to the garage they were given these items by the local police and then began their own search for any clues which might help. But first, since nothing had been moved apart from the body, they decided to reconstruct the crime. The local detective inspector persuaded Mr Hall, the licensee of the pub next door, to play the part of the corpse and he was placed in the same position as the body was found. A trilby hat had been found near Messiter's head, and to give a touch of realism for photographic purposes, Sergeant Young placed his own hat beside the recumbent figure of Mr Hall. The detectives noted the position of several bloodstained boxes in relation to the body, some of which had been splashed to a height of several feet, an almost sure indication of blows by a heavy weapon used as a club.

John Prothero then ordered all the boxes to be moved. 'Search every nook and cranny,' he commanded. During this search three clues were found which played a vital part in the investigation.

The first was a rolled-up ball of paper, stained and begrimed with oil and dirt, lying between two oil drums near the garage door. It was a receipt for rent dated 20 October and bore the name 'Horne' of Cranbury Avenue. On the back of this scrap of paper were some faint words which obviously referred to an order for '35 or 36 gals, Tuesday' and there was a signature — 'W.F. Thomas' — the small 'O' being crossed out.

A second piece of paper was found behind another oil drum and on that was a written message. It read: 'Mr W.F. Thomas. I shall be at 42 Grove Street at 10 a.m. but not at noon. V. Messiter.'

The third clue found in the garage was a hammer, lying at the back of more oil drums against the side wall. Both the shaft and the head of the hammer were stained with blood, and stuck in the blood there was a single eyebrow hair. This last discovery changed the whole complex of the killing, for the hammer was without doubt the murder weapon. Vivian Messiter had not been shot, as had at first been suspected, but battered to death, and the small wound in the dead man's forehead had not been caused by a bullet but by a ferocious blow from the pointed side of the hammer head.

The pathologist Sir Bernard Spilsbury was called in, and while the Yard men waited for him to arrive, they began to make inquiries about the other things they had found.

The landlady at Cranbury Avenue, Mrs Horne, established that she had recently had a quiet, well-behaved couple staying there for about two weeks. Their names were Mr and Mrs Thomas and they had left on 3 November, leaving an address care of Allied Transport Co., 38 High Road, Chiswick.

The Chiswick police checked and found there was no firm of that name and, moreover, there was no house in the High Road bearing that number. Further checks relating to names and addresses on the other scraps of paper found in the garage revealed there was no Bold Street in Southampton, nor any firm bearing the name Cromer & Bartlett. There was no such place as Clayton Farm anywhere near Winchester, while Ben Jervis had never been heard of at Crescent Bassett.

It began to look as though Mr W.F. Thomas

was at least a liar and it did prove he had some connection with the murdered man. The only thing so far proved genuine was the signature of H.H. Galton, and it looked as though it had been deliberately left in the memorandum book to make him a suspect, for Mr Galton was traced and proved to be a genuine customer.

Messiter's lodgings were in Carlton Road, and among the papers he had left behind was a letter bearing the address of Cranbury Avenue and signed 'W.F. Thomas'. The writer was applying for an agency with Messiter in reply to an advertisement which the latter had inserted in the *Southern Daily Echo*. This was another link between Thomas and Messiter, but where was Thomas?

Prothero issued a full description of Thomas to the press, mentioning a small scar on his face. Newspapers always like a dramatic headline and so the hunt for Thomas became 'Hunt for Man with a Scar'.

Five days after the discovery of the crime Bernard Spilsbury went to Southampton and examined the body of the victim. He described his findings: 'At least three blows on the head, any one producing immediate unconsciousness. The head of a large hammer, used with great violence, would account for injuries. Those across base and on right side produced when the head was on a hard surface. Position of injuries at back suggest that deceased was bending forwards. Puncture wounds on top of head — striking edge of tin box in fall.'

The Yard men went over the information they had and came to the conclusion that the man they wanted was cunning enough to be no stranger to crime, as evinced by his inventing bogus orders to get commission; his flight from one place to another; the tearing out of what were probably incriminating pages from the books found in the garage; and the adroit way he had tried to cover his tracks. Sergeant Young suggested to his chief that the man might have a record.

'Send for Battley,' Prothero said. A call to the Yard brought Detective Inspector Harry Battley, then head of the Fingerprint Bureau, to Southampton and with him he brought all the files in the name of Thomas. There were eighty-three dossiers.

Battley examined the hammer and the shaft and all the other finds but there were no useful fingerprints. All the files holding photographs of men called Thomas were shown to the landlady, Mrs Horne, and to various other people who might have recognized him. But not one person was able to pair up a photograph and the missing man.

The investigation seemed to be running down when luck took a hand. The Wiltshire police, who had seen the circulated description of W.F. Thomas, sent a message that they were looking for a man with the same name. This man had worked for a building contractor named Mitchell at Downton, near Salisbury. Thomas had entered the employ of Mr Mitchell on 3 November 1928 (the day Thomas had left his Cranbury Avenue lodgings) and had disappeared with more than £130 of his employer's money on 21 December. He had given as his previous employers the Allied Transport Road Association, Bold Street, Southampton.

A landlady in Downton told the police that a Mr and Mrs Thomas had lodged with her and, in a vase in the room they had occupied, was found yet another scrap of paper. It was a docket from an order book, headed: 'A & R S'.

Underneath was an address — 85 London Road, Manchester.

The piece of paper left at Downton was one piece of paper too many — it began to provide leads.

A swift inquiry was made to the Manchester police. They did not know a W.F. Thomas, but they did know Auto & Radio Services at

London Road. A detective said, 'We are looking for a man named Podmore who used to work for them. We want him for conversion of money he received for a car. His picture was in the *Police Gazette*.'

Criminal Records now came into their own. William Henry Podmore had a file, and there was no question that he and Thomas were the same person. A check on his history was revealing and began to fill in the gaps. He was well known to the Staffordshire police, having been first arrested by them when he was only eleven. He was married but parted from his wife and had been living with a young woman in various parts of the country.

At one time he had lived with his parents at Greenly Road, Abbey Milton, Stoke-on-Trent. Near his home was Bold Street, the street name which kept cropping up in the Messiter case. He had known a Mr Baskeyfield whom he always called Baskerfield, the name of the person mentioned as living at the Clayton Farm address, while a Mr Albert Machen, who actually lived at Clayton Farm, Newcastle, Staffordshire, used to deliver milk to the Podmore family. He also knew a Mrs Lucy Jervis, although not personally.

Podmore had made the mistake common

to petty criminals, that of mixing up familiar names and places in the faint hope of appearing to be honest. It is an error that has helped to trap many people. It began to look very much as though Podmore, alias Thomas, was the man who had murdered Vivian Messiter. But proof was still lacking. Prothero decided to concentrate his search for the woman companion who was called 'Lil'.

Inquiries at Podmore's home revealed that he had stayed there over Christmas and had left early in the New Year to take a job as a garage hand at the Stonebridge Hotel, Solihull, near Birmingham. He had arrived there on 5 January 1929 with his 'wife', Lil, who was to work as a cook. Six days later, when the evening papers printed the reports of the Southampton garage murder, Podmore handed in his notice, saying he wanted to leave at once. Next day Podmore and Lil departed without even asking for their wages. Podmore obviously thought that Lil, called 'Golden-haired Lil' in the Press, was an embarrassment, and that it was no longer safe for them to be seen together. The first signs of panic had set in, and he sent her back to her home at Stoke-on-Trent. There she was interviewed by the local detective inspector, Mr Diggle, who had been making all the inquiries in Staffordshire. She told him she thought it likely that Podmore would have gone to the Leicester Hotel in Vauxhall Bridge Road, near Victoria in London.

Two telephone calls, one to Southampton and one from there to the Yard, had Detective Charles Simmons with a sergeant casually leaning against the reception desk of the Leicester Hotel asking quietly for 'Mr Thomas' or 'Mr Podmore'. He was in his room and agreed to accompany the officers to Southampton. Under the circumstances refusal would have been difficult although, in truth, there was little evidence of murder against him at the time.

On 18 January, just eight days after the finding of Messiter's body, Podmore met for the first time the two men who had been hunting him, Detective Chief Inspector John Prothero and Detective Sergeant Hugh Young. Podmore was nonchalant, almost cocksure. Prothero was his usual calm, gentlemanly self, and Young sat at a table, pen in hand and a pad of statement forms in front of him, the classic reception for all suspects.

It was clear that Podmore had been through this routine before and was fairly confident. It was also clear that he was not going to give in without a struggle. He admitted he was in trouble in Manchester and in Downton and that he had worked for

Messiter. He had seen the report of the finding of Messiter's body. He was completely frank about using the names of Thomas and Podmore. He said he went to see Messiter on the morning of 30 October and that also there was an agent named Maxton or Baxton, a subtle suggestion that this was the man who had killed Messiter. He had only seen him once but he did not need pressing to give a description. Details of the man's height, build, hair, complexion and clothing rolled off his tongue in almost indecent haste.

Podmore said he had left Messiter's employ for a better job with Mr Mitchell at Salisbury. He admitted taking Messiter's car to go for the interview at Downton on 30 October, the last day on which Messiter was seen alive, and said that he had returned at 4.30 p.m. that day, parked the car in the garage and gone to his lodgings.

In its way this was a helpful admission. Unless someone else could be found who had seen Messiter later, Podmore was the last person to have seen him alive.

There was one obvious motive for the murder in Podmore's case — the bogus orders in equally bogus names and addresses — an easy way to get commission on non-existent sales of oil. And if Messiter had

46

found out and challenged Podmore, what then?

Podmore was held in custody. This caused no problems to the Yard men, since he was already wanted for other offences. Meanwhile luck again turned in favour of the detectives. They had circulated a description of the hammer to the newspapers and a Mr Marsh came forward to say the hammer was his. He had bought it in France and was able to recognize it because it had been 'touched up and filed down' by him. He remembered that at some time around 29 October a man with a scar on his face, who looked like a mechanic, had come to the motor works in Southampton where Marsh worked and asked to borrow a hammer. It was never returned.

Podmore blandly denied he had ever borrowed a hammer.

The case looked like breaking. Podmore was put up for identification with several other men of similar age, build and appearance and Mr Marsh walked quietly along the line. It is one of the nightmare moments in the life of a suspect. The parade was held in the yard of Bathgate police station with a uniformed inspector in charge. The Yard men stood well away. It was explained to Podmore, before the men formed themselves into line, that he could stand anywhere he chose.

It is a time for the mind to race. Which is the best place? Which of these men looks most like me? Which is wearing similar clothes? For the policemen it is slow, inexorable and ordinary. To the suspect it is mounting panic. 'Will the expression on my face reveal my guilty knowledge?'

Mr Marsh tried hard. Three times he walked up and down the line and, in the end, shook his head.

'The man is not there,' he said.

The volunteers departed and a relieved Podmore went back to the cells. Soon afterwards he was arrested by the Manchester police for theft of a car and he was sentenced to six months' imprisonment. For a while he was away from the attention of the Yard men, but he was not far away and not for long. Two months later he was brought from prison to attend the resumed inquest on Messiter, which had been formally opened and adjourned. He sat between two prison officers but was able to smile and wave at 'Golden-haired Lil' who was also in court.

Only one red herring was trailed across the path of justice, when a man serving a sentence in Winchester prison was called as a witness. He had previously made a statement

48

that a woman he knew had returned home at 2.30 p.m. on 30 October in Southampton with blood all over her face. But before the coroner he admitted his story was pure invention.

During the inquest the exercise book containing the receipt from Mr Galton for 2s 6d was produced and handed to the jury, as were the two sheets of carbon paper found in the duplicate order book. The jury returned an open verdict, Podmore went back to prison to serve the rest of his sentence, and the Yard men took away the exhibits to carry on the investigation. They went back to the Murder Room at Scotland Yard and analyzed every bit of information they had collected. Prothero, Young and Battley debated the case for hours. Then Prothero picked up the exercise book and sauntered across to the window overlooking the Thames. They had nothing in mind but it was as though they were willing this tatty, torn book to yield up its secret. They looked again at the pages they had scrutinized so many times before. Then, as Prothero held the book up in the light, a ray of sunlight, striking the paper slantwise, threw up in relief the shadowy outline of some writing. It was not the actual writing itself, only the faint impression left on the page underneath the one which had been torn out, and on which the message had been written.

When photographed the shadowy words read: 'October 28, 1928. Received from Wolf Head Oil Company commission on Cromer and Bartlett, 5 gals 5/6 commission 2/6. W.F.T.'

Comparison handwriting tests proved that this message had been written by Thomas, alias Podmore.

This now proved, beyond doubt, that Podmore had been swindling his employer, Mr Messiter. And it proved that the page from the exercise book had been torn out with Podmore's own hand. If he was the murderer he would have had good reason to destroy every bit of written evidence which connected him with Messiter. If, on the other hand, somebody other than Podmore was the murderer, what possible motive could he have had in tearing out the pages showing details of the transaction between himself and Messiter?

Still the authorities hesitated to bring a charge of murder and still Podmore remained in prison. When he finished the first sentence for the Manchester offence he received another six months for stealing money from Downton. This rather Micawberish attitude may have been influenced by the verdict of the coroner's jury. What would have happened had not Podmore been safely in custody is an interesting conjecture. But something more did turn up; two of Podmore's fellow-prisoners in Wandsworth reported statements made by him, and one of these amounted to a confession. The man's name was Cummings and he gave a statement to Prothero and Young. That was in October, and on 17 December 1929, the Yard men were waiting outside the gates of Wandsworth Prison.

In accordance with regulations, a prisoner must first be released and the new arrest made outside the prison gates. Podmore walked out with his usual jaunty air. Perhaps he felt confident he had covered all his tracks and that he had nothing to fear. Then a handcuff was locked round one of his wrists. The other handcuff was already round the wrist of Sergeant Young and Podmore was taken back to Southampton to be charged with murder.

He was tried at Winchester Assizes in March 1930, fifteen months after the crime, before the Lord Chief Justice, Lord Hewart. He was convicted, and his appeal against conviction was dismissed. An attempt to take the case to the House of Lords failed and Podmore was hanged on 22 April.

51

There was some agitation by well-meaning people to alter the course of the law because of the delay in bringing to trial and because two convicted criminals had been called to give evidence. They shared the common misunderstanding of the value of circumstantial evidence. In the volume on the case in the *Famous Trials* series the authors, one of them a lawyer, pointed out that the case against Podmore rested not only on what was found, but on what was not found.

Had the books been unmutilated, had the missing invoice and the missing receipt been there, they would have established a case of swindling against the prisoner, but it is more than doubtful whether any jury would have held that they established more — it is a very long step from false pretence to wilful murder. But they were not there, and there could have been but one hand that removed them — the hand of the man who had fabricated the orders and signed the receipt. And that removal must have taken place after Messiter's death, for before it would have been useless. That was the evidence that really convicted Podmore.

There can be no doubt that Messiter discovered the swindle and taxed Podmore with it, threatening to call the police. If it had been Podmore's first offence he would have had no cause for undue concern. But he was already wanted by the police in Manchester. Podmore, who had never before used violence, lost his temper. The hammer was there, maybe in Podmore's pocket, certainly to hand, and Messiter was struck down. The worst feature of the attack was that while the unconscious man lay on the concrete floor his assailant rained more blows on him. That callous behaviour must have told on the jury, and so must his actions immediately afterwards. For Podmore admitted that he had locked the garage and taken Messiter's car to give his lady friend, 'Golden-haired Lil', a drive and 'some fresh air'.

THE POISONER

(Kenneth Barlow, UK 1957)

Percy Hoskins

The first murder case in Britain in which the weapon was said to be insulin, the drug used to treat diabetes. Kenneth Barlow was a male nurse who claimed that insulin was the key to the perfect murder, since once it dissolved in the bloodstream it was untraceable. When his wife Elizabeth was found dead in her bath, a doctor noticed puncture marks on her skin. Samples from her body, tested on mice, led to the detection of insulin. In a ground-breaking experiment, a team of forensic scientists discovered that lactic acid which had formed in Mrs Barlow's muscles after death had prevented the breakdown of insulin. Barlow broke down while being interviewed by detectives. While he denied injecting his wife with insulin, he claimed he'd actually injected her with ergometrine in an effort to induce an abortion. In fact no abortifacient drugs were found in Mrs Barlow's body. Doctors, scientists and biochemists all gave conflicting evidence at Barlow's trial. The defence theory was that Mrs Barlow had fainted in the bath, causing a massive and fatal dose of insulin to be released into the bloodstream. But the jury was not persuaded, and Barlow was convicted and sentenced to life imprisonment. The legendary crime reporter Percy Hoskins (1904–89) joined the Daily Express in 1928. He is best remembered for his work on the 1956 case of John Bodkin Adams, the Eastbourne doctor accused of killing rich, elderly patients in order to collect from their wills. Hoskins was the only Fleet Street journalist convinced of Adams' innocence, and reported accordingly to the Express. He also assisted in the doctor's defence. Adams was acquitted in 1957, the year in which the Barlow case occurred.

Poison lends itself most conveniently to the dream of perfect murder. Use a gun, and the commotion will bring every copper for miles around, and the tell-tale mark of the firing pin is as damning as any fingerprint.

Strangle, and the pathologist will find you out, even if you fake murder to look like suicide by hanging and bury the body afterwards.

Chop the victim into pieces, dismember, drop the segments in tightly wrapped parcels into the sea and still the Murder Squad will triumph: witness the human wild animal called Hume caged in his Swiss prison.

Do what you will to escape detection: burn the body; suffocate; rain blows on the skull from behind; electrocute; knife; destroy the whole human frame, bones and all, in a tank full of acid; hide the corpse so well no man will ever set eyes on it again; push it through a ship's porthole and feed it to the sharks (as James Camb did to 'Gay' Gibson) and even then stand trial for murder.

But poison: there you have a chance to get off scot-free. It is so easy to administer. The victim is hungry or thirsty and, in any case, unsuspecting.

And, if you do your homework sufficiently well, you may hit upon a poison that leaves no trace at all. I know of one, not too difficult to obtain, where the apparent effect is one of heart failure . . . with no trace of poison left in the system. That is the great attraction of poison to the murderer: the protection afforded by its worm-like stealth.

There are others. It is a weapon well suited to the weak, hence its popularity with women. And it is a joy to possess and use if you hate someone enough: of all methods of murder, here is the most painful, sly, and cruel. Poisons like arsenic, the commonest and easiest to obtain, guarantee a monstrously agonizing end.

For all these reasons, poison has been a popular method of killing since the time of the Borgias. What is rare is to find motiveless poisoning. It seems inconceivable that any man should plan murder this way merely to see if it can pass undetected — or does it?

Of all the cases that have come my way in this specialized field of poison, the Barlow case rates a mention on two counts. He committed the first known case of murder through injection of insulin — his wife was a non-diabetic, so it led to her collapse and drowning in the bath — and he did it for no reason anyone can discover. The only conclusion I can draw from the known facts is that he believed he could get away with murder by insulin and experimented accordingly.

Kenneth Barlow, aged thirty-eight, lived with his wife Elizabeth in a terraced two-up and two-down in Thornbury Crescent, Bradford, in Yorkshire. He was a male nurse and worked in St Luke's Hospital in the West Riding town of Huddersfield. She had a local job, in a laundry. They had been married less than a year. They seemed to be ideally happy.

The neighbours found them a happy and apparently easy-going pair.

On the night of 3 May, 1957, between 11 p.m. and midnight, Kenneth Barlow hammered on his neighbour's door and shouted to them to call the doctor — *quickly*. He said his wife had passed out in the bath, and he had found her with her head under water; he had tried artificial respiration without success. Then he ran back indoors, to continue artificial respiration, until the doctor arrived.

Barlow had his story off pat when first the doctor and then an observant Detective Sergeant called Naylor from Bradford CID called round. His wife was tired that night, said Barlow, and had gone to bed early. He put the child (from his previous marriage) to bed himself, went round and locked up in the normal way, and went upstairs some time later.

About 10 p.m. Mrs Barlow, who had complained of the heat, said she now felt better and was going to take a bath. Right, said Kenneth Barlow, and promptly dozed off: came to about 11 p.m., found his wife had not come back to bed, then noticed the light still on in the bathroom. He went in to find her unconscious, with her head well under water. He pulled the plug out at once and began to administer first aid. Now he stood in the hallway, cool and composed although naturally sad, to greet doctor and detective as they arrived.

Both of them noticed how the pupils of her eyes were dilated, as though she were under the influence of some drug. Sergeant Naylor also spotted one curious thing: Barlow's pyjamas were bone dry, although — on his own admission — he was wearing them when he tried to revive poor Elizabeth Barlow. The alarm bells that ring to warn every good policeman things are not as straightforward as they seem sounded that night in the house in Thornbury Crescent, and Naylor called his superiors right away.

The Chief Constable of Bradford, Mr H. S. Price, went to the house. He looked at the body. He too was baffled by those dry pyjamas and another factor: lack of water on the walls and floor. Curious, when the bath was full enough to drown Mrs Barlow, that the attempts to lift her out and give artificial respiration had not even left one puddle on the bathroom floor.

He called in Dr David Price, the West Riding pathologist and the senior inspector from the Harrogate laboratories. Dilation of the pupils seemed a sure indication that Mrs Barlow was drugged when she died. The police found syringes in the house, but

Barlow was a male nurse and his story that he had used one to give himself penicillin for a carbuncle on the neck seemed reasonable.

The body was taken to the mortuary for post mortem and extensive tests for poisons and drugs. More scientists were called in next day but immediate tests again showed nothing traceable in the system. What Dr Price did find, however, were four tiny red dots in the buttocks similar to marks left by hypodermic injection. He cut away the flesh around and below both sets of punctures and ascertained that they had been made shortly before her collapse and death in the bath.

More specialists were called in for consultation: Professor C. S. Russell, a gynaecologist from Sheffield (Mrs Barlow was found to be in the early stages of pregnancy); Professor Thompson, from Guy's Hospital in London; and a senior chemist from Boots' factory at Nottingham. They had to weigh the symptoms shown by Mrs Barlow before death — including her collapse before sliding under the level of the bathwater.

Insulin, of course, is not a poison in the sense that arsenic is. It is extensively used in the treatment of diabetics to reduce the sugar content of the blood. If it is injected into a non-diabetic, that person goes into a state of shock and collapse. So, if the bath should be

60

full enough, such a fainting fit could well prove fatal.

Insulin? There was no known case of injection by insulin in the course of murder. Here was a completely virgin field of research for the combined Murder Squad — police backed by the scientists. While Dr Price and his colleagues concentrated on laboratory experiments, the police stepped up their inquiries into Barlow's background.

In the laboratory, samples taken from the flesh cut away from Mrs Barlow's body were injected into mice. Other mice were injected with insulin. The results were identical. The creatures went into a state of collapse and died. Guinea pigs were used in the same way with the same result. The human tissues were then injected with anti-insulin compounds and used again on the mice and guinea pigs, but this time, with the insulin destroyed deliberately, there were no ill effects. So it *was* insulin that was used to murder Mrs Barlow.

In the CID headquarters at Bradford every precaution was taken not to forewarn Barlow of their line of inquiry. Discreet checks were made at the hospital where he worked to see what medicines and drugs he had access to, and how much — if any — was unaccounted for. There was professional evidence aplenty that he often gave injections of insulin to patients.

Barlow was charged with the murder of his wife. All through the period of arrest and trial he protested his innocence.

Sir Harry Hylton-Foster, then Solicitor-General, led the prosecution. It is not the easiest of cases to take through the court, in spite of the magnificent backroom work by Dr Price and his associates.

Here you had a man and wife, known to be happy together, married less than a year. No shred of evidence as to any quarrel or bad feeling between them, no sudden blazing row that could have ended in a resolve to murder. What could the motive have been? There was no suggestion of gain. There was no hint of jealousy, no rumour of another man or woman in the marital background.

Barlow's story of how those two syringes came to be found in his house was still convincing enough. Traces of penicillin *had* been found on the one he said he used for the boil on his neck, and he said both he and his wife had used the other. She had given her father injections of morphia, he said, to ease the pain of cancer; and he had used it on her for injections of a drug called ergometrine, to end her pregnancy — at her own request.

He also said she had had fainting fits

before: once in the bath, and he described how he had rescued her just in time on that occasion.

Sir Harry called on three witnesses who had heard Barlow refer to insulin in the past as one means to the 'perfect murder'. There was male nurse Harry Stork, who had worked with Barlow in a sanatorium in the middle fifties. He recalled Barlow saying it would be difficult to detect afterwards as it dissolved in the bloodstream.

A former patient at the same sanatorium remembered a conversation with Barlow who said of insulin: 'Get a load of this, and it's the quickest way out.' Then there was a woman nurse who had tended diabetics with Barlow, and remembered him saying: 'You could kill somebody with insulin as it can't be found very easily — unless you use a very large dose.'

There was, however, a significant weakness implicit in this line of prosecution argument. Barlow had been married to Elizabeth less than one year. Was the jury to believe he was already contemplating the murder of a wife he had yet to meet?

The defence, led by Mr Bernard Gillies QC, called as their expert witness Dr Hobson, from St Luke's Hospital in London. He told the court that in moments of stress (like anger, for instance, *or fear*) the human body automatically releases and pumps adrenalin into the bloodstream. This in turn raises the sugar level — which could produce an increase of insulin as a natural reaction.

'If [Mrs Barlow] knew she was slipping down and drowning in the bath,' he said, 'and that she could not get out, she would be terrified and I think that would produce all the symptoms the chemists have described.'

Against this was the amount of insulin found below those hypodermic syringe marks in the woman's body. Insulin produced naturally in the way Dr Hobson described would be evenly distributed over the body — and it would need a fantastic amount to reach the overall level found round those puncture marks.

The judge told the jury: 'If you are satisfied he injected insulin into his wife and knowingly injected it, you will probably find no difficulty in reaching the decision that he did so with intent to kill.'

Mr Justice Diplock told them to make up their minds, saying 'This is murder or nothing'. The jury found for murder. Barlow was sentenced to life imprisonment, and a new page had been written in British criminal history.

Apart from my constant checks through

Scotland Yard, I took no part in the police investigation before Barlow was finally charged. This was a matter for my associates in the northern offices of the *Daily Express*. What fascinated me, and took me to the trial, was the knowledge that this was to be the first trial for murder by insulin injection in any murder investigation.

I have discussed the case many times since with many an expert and always our talks have ended with the one question: why did he do it?

Barlow's first wife had died in 1956 at the early age of thirty-three. Even after the inquest, doubt existed over the precise cause of her death, although it was found to be from natural causes. If his protestations of innocence at the time of his trial for the murder of Elizabeth, his second wife, were genuine, then here was someone who had been dealt a doubly cruel blow by Fate.

But if the verdict was just — that he committed 'a cold, cruel and carefully premeditated murder' as the judge said — even though he was happily married, we are left with only one possible conclusion. Here was a man who really believed he had found the way to commit the 'perfect murder' and so carried it out as a cold-blooded and clinical experiment. On his new wife, who unfortunately happened to be the most convenient human guinea pig.

If his method of murder was unique, it shows Barlow held at least one trait in common with all poisoners: a callous disregard for suffering. He would have done well in any Nazi wartime concentration camp.

THE JEKYLL AND HYDE OF NEW YORK

(Dr Arthur Waite, USA 1916)

John Laurence

Even on trial for his life, accused of double murder, Dr Arthur Warren Waite laughed at the law. It was, he agreed, all true. He had indeed murdered his mother-in-law by mixing germs in her food. He had also killed his wealthy father-in-law, but when the germs failed, and arsenic too, Waite had used chloroform, suffocating the old man with a pillow to finish him off. Why? 'For the money' said Waite. His trial was the New York sensation of its day. The debonair young dentist cheerfully explained how he had poisoned his mother-in-law mixing pneumonia, diphtheria and influenza germs into her meals. Waite's father-in-law had been a hardier soul, resisting tuberculosis bacteria sprayed up his nose, chlorine gas, and various attempts to give him pneumonia, including dampening his sheets. Science caught up with Dr Waite when arsenic he'd poured into the old man's soup was detected at the autopsy.

Doctor Arthur Warren Waite, dentist and crack tennis player, to all outward seeming was a child of fortune. He had everything the normal man wants and envies in others, good looks, charm of manner, athletic abilities, a charming wife, and a millionaire father-in-law.

Let us particularize. In appearance Doctor Waite was the typical athletic American, clean-shaven, clear-eyed, regular-featured and frankly healthy. He was popular with men and women alike, and all with whom he came in contact trusted him. He was always perfectly groomed and had that *savoir faire* which comes from wide travel. A witty conversationalist, he could talk entertainingly on most subjects, and he was much in demand by the hostesses of New York.

His father-in-law was John E. Peck, a retired millionaire druggist of Grand Rapids, Michigan, of which town Waite himself was a native. Waite's parents were not well-to-do, but their son showed such brilliance and promise that he was encouraged in every possible way to obtain the best education which they could afford. He went to the

University of Michigan and there took a dental course.

From there the brilliant student went to London and afterwards to South Africa, where he did a certain amount of practice in the profession for which he had been trained. Shortly after the outbreak of the Great War he returned to the United States and to his native town. There he met Miss Clara Peck. In spite of the wide gulf between their financial positions, a gulf which might almost have made people suspect he was a fortune hunter, no suggestion of the kind was made when it became known that the two were engaged. Everyone who met the good-looking dentist predicted such a successful career for him that he would never be in any financial difficulties.

Clara Peck and Arthur Warren Waite were married at Grand Rapids in September, 1915. To the surprise of many, however, he did not begin practising there, but moved at once to New York on the plea that the opportunities for advancement were much greater in that town, and his newly-married wife would have greater chances of amusement.

Waite was in no hurry to begin practising. He had always shown a great interest in medicine, and within a few days of arriving in

New York he had got in touch with a number of doctors whom he deluded into believing he was a fully-qualified man himself, wealthy, and interested in scientific research, especially the study of bacteriology.

A certain amount of verisimilitude was given to Waite's story by the fact that he had a flat in the exclusive Riverside Drive Apartments, a flat which was richly furnished. The doctor was also well-known as a very good amateur tennis player who had only recently taken part in a number of tournaments at Palm Beach, Florida. He had, too, a considerable amount of medical knowledge, partly acquired through his study of dentistry, and partly learnt through an instinctive desire to acquire knowledge which might prove of use to him in later years.

Through various influences Waite got in touch with Dr Percival L. de Nyce, who was in charge of the bacteriological laboratory of the Flower Hospital, one of the best known institutions in New York. Dr Nyce was impressed with his new pupil, and the extraordinarily keen interest he took in all germ cultures. But it was only in the most virulent and deadly germs that his pupil was really interested, and he actually complained to Dr Nyce that the germs he was studying were not virulent enough for the experiments he had in mind!

Clara Waite firmly believed her husband was in practice as a doctor, and once or twice, in order to foster that belief and account for the necessary income to keep up their expensive style of living, he took her to the Flower Hospital and asked her to stay in the waiting room for a while. After keeping her there kicking her heels for half an hour or so, and reflecting on what he might be doing, he would return and announce that he had just finished an important operation. The deluded Clara, who understood not a single detail of the medical account her husband gave her, was full of pride that his abilities were being recognized in such an important institution.

It may well be asked at this stage, where was the comparatively poor student of a year or two ago getting the large sums of money which were necessary not only for his living expenses but for those in connection with the bacteriological experiments he was carrying out?

Waite had ingratiated himself so well with the Peck family that, with one exception, they were intensely proud of the brilliant addition to it. His wife's father helped financially so that his son-in-law should not be handicapped in any of his research work which he represented was necessary to advance in his profession. He not only gave his daughter a very handsome dowry, out of which the Riverside apartments were so luxuriously furnished, but he allowed her £60 a month.

It must be admitted that Waite had an exceedingly great attraction for women, especially for women older than himself. Mrs Peck adored him. Nothing he could do was wrong, and her sister-in-law, Miss Catherine Peck, who had given her niece a cheque for nearly a thousand pounds as a wedding present, had even a higher opinion of him. So much did she value his advice, indeed, that she was easily persuaded to let him have £10,000 of her money to invest. It was on this money that Waite lived. Aunt Catherine was unwise enough to let it be known that on her death Waite would receive a very substantial legacy. It was also common knowledge in the family that Mr Peck's will left half his fortune to his daughter Clara. If Mr and Mrs Peck died, and Aunt Catherine died, and perhaps later on Clara Waite, Arthur Warren Waite would be a very rich and eligible widower!

A few weeks after their arrival in New York the devoted young husband — and there was not the slightest doubt that to all outward appearances he was infatuated with his young wife — suggested that her mother and father should be asked to stay with them for a while. Both parents were delighted to accept their son-in-law's invitation, but neither stayed very long on this first visit, for the air of New York did not seem to agree with Mr Peck. He felt run down almost as soon as he arrived. His son-in-law diagnosed a coming cold and sprayed his throat every evening. But that did not ward off the feeling of lassitude, any more than did the medicine which Waite had made up, and Mr Peck returned to Grand Rapids to be thoroughly overhauled there by his own doctors. They confessed themselves completely puzzled. However the air of Grand Rapids certainly suited old Mr Peck better than did that of New York and he was soon feeling as fit as ever.

Mrs Peck had found the visit to her beloved daughter and son-in-law all too short and as soon as she was satisfied that her husband was on the road to recovery and not likely to have a relapse, she paid them another visit — her last. Shortly after her arrival, she, too, began to feel ill, and a Doctor Porter was called in. He diagnosed that there was nothing very much the matter, though Dr Waite strongly disagreed, and asserted that he was sure his mother-in-law was seriously ill.

One night when Dr Waite was out ostensibly visiting his patients, a very remarkable incident occurred, though no one thought much about it at the time. Mrs Waite, who had gone to bed, detected a strong smell of gas and traced it as coming from her mother's room. When she entered it she found that the tap of the gas stove had been left on and if it had not been for the fact one of the windows was partly open there is no doubt her mother would have been asphyxiated.

From that day, however, Mrs Peck grew steadily worse, and on January 30th, 1916, she died. Doctor Porter, who had suspected nothing wrong, readily gave his certificate. Dr Waite, who seemed utterly grief-stricken by his mother-in-law's sudden death, accompanied her body to Grand Rapids, where he told various members of the family that her last dying wish was that she should be cremated. The ashes were buried in the family vault. The act of cremation had effectively destroyed all danger of anyone finding out the real cause of the old lady's death.

Mr Peck was overwhelmed by the loss of his wife and in February he accepted a second invitation to come to New York to visit his daughter. Both he and Clara had been very fond of Mrs Peck and both were eager to be together in their common sorrow. Old Mr Peck, too, liked his son-in-law, for the latter had been more sympathetic than even a devoted son-in-law might be expected to be. Waite was so charming, so anxious to make his father-in-law forget, so full of warmth on the old man's arrival, that for a few days Mr Peck really was cheered up and felt far less lonely than he had been feeling since his wife's death. There was a very strong bond of affection between his daughter and himself, for in her he saw again the mother as she was in the days when he first courted her and began his successful struggle for fortune.

During those early days of Mr Peck's second visit to the Riverside Apartment there occurred an incident which has a considerable bearing on the rest of the story. Dr Waite, as far as his devoted wife Clara knew, and her father knew, was an exceedingly busy man. He had to be out many evenings visiting his patients, and sometimes he was so hard-pressed that he did not return until the early hours of the morning. Actually Waite was very fond of wine, women and song. He had early discovered that he exercised a peculiar influence over women, and his life in New York was a continual round of gaiety. Although the delightful doctor distributed his favours on a fairly lavish scale, entertaining at the most expensive restaurants and dance cafés those whom he favoured, there was one lady in particular who proved more attractive than the rest, a Mrs Horton.

Margaret Horton, a beautiful young grass widow, had met Waite first at the Berlitz School of Languages. She was ambitious to become an opera singer. In a few days Waite had installed her in a suite of rooms at the Hotel Plaza. He himself was very fond of music and the two proved very congenial company for one another.

'Dr Waite had an extraordinary kind heart,' she said some months after their first meeting. 'He loved all the fine sentiments and the beautiful things of life. He used to say to me, 'Margaret, when you sing you make me weep, because you make me think of beautiful things'. He loved music. It was that love of music which drew us together.'

It was while dining with Margaret Horton that Waite was seen by a Doctor Cornell, a relative of the Peck family, and a Miss Hardwicke. When Waite saw Cornell he made an excuse to his companion and walked across to the other table. He explained glibly that he had just completed an important operation.

'I have brought my own special nurse with

me for dinner as I felt that she deserved something out of the ordinary for her skill and devotion to my work,' he explained.

He told his story with easy confidence and all those at the table, with the exception of Miss Hardwicke, were inclined to believe it. But she had been watching Waite and Margaret Horton, and she was secretly convinced that there was a deeper relationship between the two than that of doctor and nurse. But she made no outward comment, though the time was soon to come when she was to crystallize her suspicions into such drastic action that Waite's name, in consequence, was to fill the front pages of the American newspapers for many a long day.

A few days after the incident in the restaurant Mr Peck was taken seriously ill and a Dr Moore was called in. He diagnosed digestive trouble and prescribed accordingly. Mr Peck's son-in-law was most attentive. The sick man did not like his medicine and Dr Waite soon found a way out of the difficulty. One evening Waite came into the kitchen and without any disguise poured some medicine into his father-in-law's soup. Later in the evening he came into the kitchen again when tea was being prepared for Mr Peck and poured some further medicine into the teapot.

'Dora,' he explained to the servant, 'father didn't like his soup, so I must put some more medicine in his tea.'

Although Dr Moore had not considered the condition of his patient to be very serious, Dr Waite, as in the case of Mrs Peck, disagreed with him.

'He hasn't a very strong constitution,' he declared, 'and I should not be surprised if he did not live for long.'

As with Mrs Peck, Waite's prophecy proved more accurate than had that of other doctors. On March 12th, but six weeks after his wife's death, Mr Peck died, and Clara Waite had lost both her parents. And as with the case of Mrs Peck, Waite declared that his father-in-law's last wish was that he should be cremated and his ashes placed beside those of his wife. Accordingly, the body, accompanied by the grief-stricken Clara and her sorrowing husband, was taken to Grand Rapids for that purpose. Before that journey, however, the body had been embalmed, a fact which should be borne in mind.

To Dr Waite's astonishment he found when he got to Grand Rapids that the family were not in favour of the old man being cremated. He was careful enough, however, not to raise any great objections, and after duly seeing his father-in-law buried he hurried back to New

York — and Mrs Horton. Of late he had been spending money freely, too freely, but now, under his father-in-law's will, through Clara, he would have no cause to worry about money for some time. When he had, there was always Miss Catherine Peck, who had promised him a substantial legacy on her death.

There was one member of the Peck family who had never been very friendly with Dr Waite, who had always disliked him in fact, despite his great charm. That was Percival Peck, Clara's only brother. It was Percival Peck who had raised the greatest objections to his father being cremated. Just before the arrival of the body at Grand Rapids he had received a mysterious telegram from New York which read as follows: 'Suspicions aroused. Demand autopsy. Keep telegram secret. — K. Adams.'

The name of Adams was quite unknown to Percival Peck, but that fact did not influence him in the least. It transpired afterwards that K. Adams was the Miss Hardwicke who had seen Dr Waite and Mrs Horton dining together, and who had disbelieved the story the former told that the lady was his nurse. But the telegram, from whatever source it came, provided young Peck with an opportunity which he eagerly seized. He had a secret examination made of his father's body and at the same time employed private detectives to keep an eye on his brother-in-law and keep a record of his movements.

Clara, who had become seriously ill following upon the double shock of her mother's and father's deaths, had stayed behind at Grand Rapids, while her husband had hurried back to the gaieties of New York.

And then Waite received his first shock. He had left Grand Rapids fully satisfied that he had bluffed everyone, that he could now spend money just as freely as he wished, enjoy himself to the top of his bent. But a few days after his return Mr Peck's son-in-law received a shock. The undertaker who had arranged for the embalming of Mr Peck called upon him and asked that his bill should be paid.

'What's the hurry?' asked Waite. 'You know the money is safe enough, don't you?'

He was surprised at the sudden demand for the bill, but he was more than surprised by the undertaker's reply. It worried him. It was the tiny black cloud on the edge of the horizon.

'It's really Mr Kane, sir, the embalmer,' explained the undertaker. 'He thinks he might not get his money.'

'Why?' demanded Waite, struck by the

uneasy look in the other's face.

'Well, there's some idea that arsenic had been used,' explained the undertaker.

Waite was well aware that it was against the law for arsenic to be used in any embalming fluid, as he was also aware that arsenic would be found in Mr Peck's body if it were examined.

'I think I'd better see Mr Kane,' he said evenly.

When the doctor saw Kane he did not beat about the bush.

'How much is it worth to you to say that you used arsenic?' he asked.

The embalmer named a sum, and after some haggling Waite agreed to pay him $9,000. But Kane's nerve broke at the last minute and he told a remarkable story to the police when questioned.

'Waite told me he was in a hole and asked me to put arsenic in the sample of embalming fluid I was to give the District Attorney. He said he would make me independent for life if I did what I was asked.'

Waite by now suspected that his movements were being watched and he arranged for Kane to meet him casually in a cigar store.

'I met him there by a telephone booth,' Kane related. 'And he gave me a big roll of

81

bills. I was so scared that I could hardly tell where I was. I stood there with the money in my hand.

' 'For God's sake get that stuff out of sight,' Dr Waite said, 'and get the sample down to the District Attorney's office.'

'I went right home; I was so nervous that I couldn't count the money. I tried afterwards and couldn't do it. I put it in a bureau drawer. I was so nervous about the money that my wife noticed it. She got to worrying me and at last made me go to a doctor to find out if I was sick. I knew all right, but I didn't tell her. I shook like a leaf every now and then when I got to thinking about the money in the bureau drawer. Then I took it down to Greenport and buried it. I didn't put anything into the sample of my embalming fluid. I made up the sample just as I always make the fluid.'

Kane's own record wasn't of the best. He had been suspected on more than one occasion of helping clients 'who were in a hole' out of it on the payment of a reasonably large sum. But for the fact that Percival Peck had brought pressure to bear with the authorities and had had his own private detectives following his brother-in-law, the interview between Kane and Waite and the handing over of a large sum of money in the cigar store might not have been known until too late. But within a very short time of the meeting, it had been reported to the police, and Kane was asked for the sample of his fluid. Rumours were flying about, and it was these rumours coming to his ears which made him break down. He had embalmed the body of Mr Peck before it had been conveyed to Grand Rapids and he was now beginning to realize that there was trouble ahead. And this wouldn't be the first time he had been in trouble.

The District Attorney's suspicions had been aroused on receiving a report from Professor Vaughan, of the University of Michigan, who had made an examination of Mr Peck's body. He had sent in a report to the effect that the millionaire had died from arsenic poisoning. There was just a possibility that the arsenic had been in the embalming fluid, but when he heard Kane's story he immediately issued a warrant for the arrest of Waite.

The iron nerve of the suspected man was breaking fast under the strain of waiting, and it broke a few hours before the detectives called at his Riverside Apartments with the warrant for his arrest. He was found unconscious in the room adjoining that in which Mr and Mrs Peck had died.

But Waite was not to evade the law so easily. He was rushed to the hospital and strong emetics administered. In the hands of skilful physicians he made a rapid recovery. While he was getting over the effect of the drugs he had taken, however, he was thinking out what story to tell. He was now fully aware of the likely evidence against him and only a miracle could save him. He decided to play the part of Dr Jekyll and Mr Hyde.

When questioned by the District Attorney in hospital Waite at once admitted that he had given his father-in-law arsenic.

'Have you any accomplices?'

'Only this other fellow,' replied the accused man with elaborate carelessness.

'What other fellow?'

'The man from Egypt. He's always been inside me ever since I can remember. He has made me do things against my will. He made me take up the study of germs, as if I used them I wouldn't be detected. I was compelled against my will to put them in my father-in-law's food. Try as I would I could not get rid of my murderous other self. Often I have gone for long walks and fought against the evil one, and tried to run away from him. But he was so fleet of foot that he always caught me up.'

So earnestly did Waite tell his story that it

was partly believed.

'Did this Egyptian make you kill Mr Peck?' he was asked.

'When my father-in-law came to stay with us I wanted to help him all I could. Then the man from Egypt said Mr Peck was too old to live, that he ought to die, and if he did die I wouldn't have to worry about money. He brushed aside all my arguments. When Mr. Peck had first visited us the Egyptian made me spray his throat with germs, but though they made him ill they did not kill him. I was ordered this time to use arsenic as it was quicker. I was told to put it in his soup and tea and egg nog. I did my best, but the Egyptian was in control. Try as I could I found it impossible to get rid of him. But now that he has forced me to do these things he has left me, and for the first time I felt that my soul is free. He seemed to leave me last night and he hasn't returned again to-day to torture me with his evil suggestions.'

The story told by Waite had exactly the effect he foresaw. It was so wild that it seemed as though only a madman could tell it. Some of the leading alienists in America were called in by the prosecution as well as by the defence.

Dr Jeliffe, the leading alienist for the prosecution, said at the trial, 'In my opinion the prisoner was sane and knew the nature and quality of his act. He was fully aware of all the phases of his crime. In my opinion he is an average man, somewhat superficial, inclined to be snobbish and of no great intellectual attainments.'

With that a number of other leading doctors agreed and ultimately their opinion prevailed.

While he was waiting his trial an amazing story came to light. Some of this has already been told. A search of Waite's flat resulted in the discovery of a number of books on poisons and a hundred and eighty slides containing germs of tetanus (lockjaw), typhoid, diphtheria, cholera and other deadly diseases with which he had been experimenting. He had spent large sums on women and amusement and had given Mrs Horton jewellery which had been entrusted to him by Miss Catherine Peck. Practically all the money the latter had given him to invest had gone in riotous living. Only the death of his father-in-law, indeed, could save him from exposure and ruin. So cunningly had he disguised his various amours that until he was arrested his wife had no knowledge of them.

'I was so shocked and amazed that I could not believe them true,' she declared after her husband's arrest. 'It seems impossible that a man who has been so uniformly gentle and kind to me and apparently so loyal could be guilty of the crime with which he is charged.'

Dozens of people who knew Waite well were as puzzled. Many believed that he really was a Jekyll and Hyde, that he had been obsessed by the man from Egypt, as he asserted. Others asserted that the story was told deliberately in an attempt to evade the law. There was one man who never believed for one single moment that the doctor was insane. That was Percival Peck, the man who had received the mysterious telegram and acted on it so promptly, the man who at once employed private detectives to follow his brother-in-law's movements, who never ceased his efforts to unearth everything he could to prove Waite's guilt.

'I know that Arthur is guilty,' he declared shortly after Waite's arrest. 'The electric chair will be too good for him. Even if he were tortured his death would never bring back my beloved parents or pay for his horrible deeds. I will do all in my power to see that he is found guilty and executed.

'He is surely entitled to no consideration whatever. I am convinced that Dr Waite married my sister Clara with but one idea, and that was to get her money. Even before her mother died he predicted an untimely death for us all. We believed him to be a surgeon, and when mother died we suspected nothing. Even when the news of father's death came we did not suspect until I got that telegram. I am sure if it had not been for that my sister and my aunt would have died next.'

Percival Peck was adamant to the last. He approached the prosecution shortly before the trial and said:

'I have only one favour to ask, and that is that I have a seat through every minute of the trial near that man, so that I can see the last gleam of hope gradually fade from his face.'

In the witness box Waite was perfectly cool, and he made no attempt to hide the appallingly evil personality of the man from Egypt who had compelled him to commit and contemplate crimes which shocked even New York. The more terrible his story, the more coolly it was told, the greater the chance the jury would believe that only a madman could do these things. His own counsel, by clever questions, brought out details of the murder of Mrs Peck and her husband which seemed to show that only a madman could have acted the way Waite did.

'What did you do after you had given your mother-in-law the fatal dose of poison?' asked his counsel.

'Why, I went to sleep, of course,' answered

the prisoner in the witness box. He added that in the morning he went along to his mother-in-law's bedroom and, finding her dead, quietly came out of the room again and waited for his wife to make the discovery her mother had died in the night. He told the jury of all the ways he had afterwards tried to kill Mr Peck before he finally succeeded.

'I gave him a throat spray and a nasal spray containing germs, and when that didn't work I got a lot of calomel which I administered to him in order to weaken him so that he could not resist the germs, but it failed. The man recovered every time. I would get him to go out and expose himself to draughts in the hope that he would catch cold, and I dampened his sheets for the same reason. Once I got some hydrochloric acid and put in the radiator in his room expecting the fumes would affect him. Finally I gave him arsenic. I sat up with him that night, as my wife was tired. He was in great pain, groaning. I gave him some chloroform and when he was unconscious I placed a pillow over his face and kept it there until he died.'

Is that the evidence of a sane man or not?

'Waite has told you the truth. There is no part of his story that is not true,' said the counsel for the defence in his final speech. 'He has no moral sense whatever. What are we going to do with such a man as this? You would not send to the electric chair an idiot, a lunatic or a child. On the other hand we cannot permit such a man as Waite to be at large. We must remove him from society by placing him in an institution.'

Mr Justice Shearn demolished the arguments of the counsel for the defence, in his address to the jury.

You are not concerned at all with the question of the punishment of this man. The question raised by defendant's counsel of what to do with such a man is not the question at all. The law determines what shall be done. Your function is to determine the facts so that the law may operate.

Don't get into your heads that you are called upon to determine anything but the facts. Juries have no right to set up standards of what constitutes right and wrong, and no right to discuss how the law shall deal with a man like this. You must not attempt to usurp the functions of the Legislature.

In this case no claim is made that the defendant did it in the heat of passion. On the contrary he himself admits premeditation, intent and a motive. No matter what the defendant has confessed you must remember the burden still rests upon the prosecution to establish his guilt beyond a reasonable doubt. The defendant is entitled to have the case determined on the facts and not on what he says.

Part of the remainder of the judge's summing up is so phrased that a copy of it should be handed to every jury in a murder case where the defence is one of insanity.

You might infer from arguments of counsel and some of the evidence that you are here to hold a medical clinic. That's not so at all. It would be absurd to ask twelve laymen to determine whether from the medical point of view a man is sane or insane, especially as men learned in the profession do not agree on the matter. The question is not whether he is sane but whether he was responsible under the tests prescribed by the law — that is, did he know the nature and quality of the act and know it was wrong. That's not a test for experts, but for men of commonsense. Moral indifference is not insanity.

The claim that the defendant was

weak in will power and that he was unable to resist suggestions like those from 'the Man from Egypt' has also been passed on by the highest courts, who have held that, no matter what medical authority there may be for such a claim, it cannot be assented to by the courts. Indulgence in evil passions weakens the will power and at the same time the sense of responsibility.

The trial was very much shorter than the great majority of sensational murder trials in America, where money can hold up justice for months. The trial only took five days and the jury were only a little over an hour bringing in their verdict of 'Guilty.'

To the last the condemned man showed that curious double personality which puzzled all those with whom he came in contact. He never wearied of talking about himself.

'My life consisted of lying, cheating, stealing and killing. My personality was that of a gentleman and I went for music, art and poetry.'

He dedicated a long poem to himself, an address to his body by his soul after death.

And thou are dead, dear comrade,
In whom I dwelt a time,

With whom I strolled through star-kissed
bowers
Of fragrant jessamine.
And thou wert weak, O comrade,
Thyself in self did fail,
And now the stars are turned to tears
And sobs the nightingale.
And though I now must leave you,
The same old songs I'll sing,
And o'er yon hill the same soft dew
Will spread its silver wing.
Across the fields, among the stars,
I now must go alone,
Your spirit now will roam afar,
And leave you, friend, alone.

A few days before his execution, when he was
reading the Bible, he remarked with his usual
charming smile, 'I was looking over the ten
Commandments and found I had broken all
but one — the one about profanity. I have
never been profane.'

He kept up his story about his two
personalities until the last.

But it did not save him. He went to his
death with that boyish smile and charming
manner which had characterized him from
the day he began his career.

THE TALKING SKULL

(Harry Dobkin, UK 1942)

Nigel Morland

A single female body unearthed amid the mass slaughter of the London Blitz was identified as a victim not of war but of a private, murderous act of mutilation — thanks to the evidence of the dead woman's dentist. Harry Dobkin, forty-nine, Russian by birth, bald, squat and bull-necked, killed his estranged wife Rachel who'd been pestering him to return to her. After crudely separating the head from the torso, Dobkin tried to remove all identifying marks, and concealed his wife's remains beneath the floor of a badly blitzed chapel. Finally, he set fire to the building under cover of enemy action, a singular deed for a man employed as a wartime fire-watcher. But the charred skeleton was discovered by chance more than a year later, and the Home Office pathologist Dr Keith Simpson reported that the unknown woman had been strangled. Her identity was established through the testimony of Mrs

94

Dobkin's dentist, who recognized the curious shape of the upper jaw as well as other features of the teeth and gums. Dobkin was convicted of murdering her and duly hanged. Nigel Morland (1905–86), one of Britain's most prolific writers of crime fact and fiction, was a co-founder of the Crime Writers' Association. After a spell as a journalist in the Far East, he edited publications as diverse as Doctor and the Edgar Wallace Mystery Magazine. He also ghosted a number of showbiz memoirs. Nigel Morland was the founder and editor of The Criminologist *and other crime-related journals including* Forensic Photography, International Journal of Forensic Dentistry *and* Current Crime.

In the greater conflagration of war it is somehow remarkably incongruous that all the vast resources of detection and justice should be devoted to the seeking and condemnation of a civilian murderer with but a single victim notched to his credit.

While thousands die on the battlefields, there is a footnote to history in a nation's trivia of homicides, yet, clearly, it is the duty of the authorities to maintain law and detect transgressions of it even if the world is falling about their ears. The pen of the historian, then, had to turn aside from the horrors of World War I, in June 1915, to record the trial of that singularly revolting, utterly worthless creature, George Joseph Smith.

And in 1942, much in the same way, part of the country paused to watch the Baptist Church murderer stand his trial while Rommel was retreating in North Africa and the Germans receded like a spent wave from the rubble-fortress of Stalingrad.

Despite the chaos of World War II, Britain's aficionados of murder could still note with interest a trial that was indeed more distinguished for the medical work contributing to its solution than for its forensic colour.

The trial was a worthy occupant of the Central Criminal Court at Old Bailey, where so much legal drama has been played out, even if it failed to reach the heights of some of its predecessors.

Chance enabled me to be present at the hearing, though it was impossible to attend on the last day, for, and it may be of faintly ironic interest, I was receiving a reprimand for putting ideas into the heads of would-be murderers. It was a sound example of how officialdom sought to guard the innocent when, in a far larger way, the innocent were being slaughtered.

It happened I had written for a newspaper a short story involving an imaginary murder during an air raid. The plot concerned a man who slew his wife by means of a piece of flak, or anti-aircraft shell, fastened to a stick and used as an edged bludgeon. It contrived a death not attributable to himself but to the rain of shell fragments which were also London's protection. The scheme was foolproof except, like all fictional (and many real) murderers, he had made a mistake by leaving the fragment at his dead wife's side still bearing the string originally tying it to the bludgeon.

An over-conscientious features editor thought this just a bit too feasible and perhaps tempting; he mentioned it casually to a Ministry of Information official, who asked me to visit him, and suggested — and no more — that it was not the best of policies to make crime *too* easy. Could I not contrive something less likely to cause possible trouble for an over-worked detective force?

Thus it was I never heard Mr Justice Wrottesley's masterly summing-up on the final day of the Baptist Church murderer's trial, but the story of the case is a veritable marvel of the medical jurist excelling fiction by conjuring from little more than dust a recognizable human being whose gruesome end was finally avenged.

* * *

The July sunshine poured through the windows of the Gordon Museum at London's Guy's Hospital, making the room warm, a heat in no way improved by a tart chemical smell and the brittle, throat-catching aroma of ancient death.

There was a brown paper parcel containing remains for the attention of Dr (later professor) Cedric Keith Simpson, noted Home Office pathologist, a parcel already familiar to him.

Its contents were first seen on 17 July 1942, when a gang of demolition workers was clearing bombed premises at 302, Upper Kennington Lane, a short distance from south London's Kennington Oval cricket ground.

Raising a stone slab in what was the cellar of a now demolished Baptist church, human remains were revealed. According to the routine of such cases, the local coroner was informed. Dr Simpson, also according to routine, saw the remains in Southwark Mortuary the following morning and was not personally satisfied they were all that was left of an air-raid victim. He thought it wise to conduct a closer examination at Guy's Hospital because of the possibly long task of trying to get some sort of identification from an incomplete skeleton bearing decaying tissues. The poor fragments, the skull entirely separated from its trunk, were bundled into a prosaic paper parcel and transported for due attention on Monday morning.

The remains were transferred to a white dust sheet and these Dr Simpson pondered before commencing what was quite a considerable task in detective work at a time when his day was filled and his leisure almost non-existent.

The first thing was visual verification of his original surmise that death had taken place some twelve or eighteen months previously;[1] that the victim was female was easily discernable by the remains of the uterus being still present.

Using camel hair brushes and loosening the tissues, the doctor began slowly, and with extreme delicacy, gradually to clean the dirt from the almost mummified remains of the body. It was exacting and wearing, the adhering dirt being not easily removed; it

---

[1] A deposit of yellowish powder over the whole was proved to be slaked lime.

required a combination of firmness and lightness, with special precautions to avoid damage to the soft tissues still remaining.

The following day saw progress add up to considerable results. It did not seem to Dr Simpson that this was an air-raid casualty. The skull had been severed cleanly from the trunk, the lower jaw was missing, and the skull also bore no scalp tissue other than a small fragment at the back — no bomb had the power to scalp and behead quite so selectively.

There were no lower portions to the arms or legs, which argued amputation. There were also marks of burning on the head, on the left side of the trunk and at the level of each knee — the left arm had been severed at the elbow joint and the right arm immediately above that joint, while the legs were separated on the left below the knee joint and at the joint on the right. The cut portions were all missing.

As a snap guess it was possible to wonder if the mutilation, and this included stripping the identifiable tissues, was the work of an unskilled person determined to hide a human identity by crude but effective methods even if, with careful disposal, she came to light some time after death.

It was without doubt a case of murder, for

the small bones of the voice box bore an injury — with bruising showing it to have been sustained in life — which Dr Simpson knew was seen only when fingers had grasped the throat and strangulation had followed.

★   ★   ★

In the busy if pedestrian professional life of a great pathologist, it is only natural that the few real puzzles which stand out from the unhappily ordinary dead are challenges to his ability and, after all, threads of colour in his more mundane daily round.

Dr Simpson knew he had before him a veritable mystery and wondered if his skill and knowledge would enable him to establish the identity of the victim, or at least sufficiently chart it for purposes of enquiry. He wanted science to give the police something sound to work on at the start of their enquiries.

The first thing to ascertain was the height of the dead woman in life. The weapon to be used was Pearson's formulae for the determination of stature, a process requiring the utmost knowledge and experience.

Reassembly of the body had revealed its stature to be about 5ft 0¼in to 5ft 0¾in, allowance being made for the missing lower legs, feet and soft tissue. Pearson's formulae, worked on the remaining long bone, the left humerus, gave height as 5ft 0½in to 5ft 1in.

The next step was to age the remains in life. This is done by checking the closure of the skull vault sutures (the zigzag markings or joints between the plates of bone in the skull vault). Here is an awkward gap from the anatomical point of view — till about twenty-five years of age the accuracy of age estimation can be achieved by several pointers in the human frame. Between that maximum and until roughly forty, there is little, except appearance, to help in closely estimating age.

But at about forty-years-old the skull vault sutures commence to close and other closures lend their aid to achieve reasonably accurate age estimates.

It was therefore possible from the skull sutures, and the closing of the palate suture (usual between 45 and 60), to settle on the approximate age of the corpse as 40 to 50; these bone fusions were remarkably helpful in Dr Simpson's reconstruction.

Colouring was proved by the fragment of scalp, to which some hairs were still attached; they were dark brown, ageing, and going grey.

There was a fibroid tumour of the uterus, a

benign growth having nothing to do with death, but possibly of value in clinching identification. Finally, there were four teeth, and some roots, remaining in the upper jaw. These had received dental attention.

This initial data Dr Simpson gave to the police with his suggestion the remains might be those of a murdered person, a woman, aged 40 to 50; she was 5ft to 5ft 1in in height, with brown hair turning gray. She suffered from a fibroid tumour of the uterus, and had possibly received medical attention for it. She had met her death some twelve to eighteen months before and, if dental records could be found, there was an upper jaw with four teeth together with their details of dental repairs, fillings, and so on available for comparison or matching.

★   ★   ★

In the meantime police enquiries had followed *their* usual routine; Divisional Detective Inspector Frederick Hatton, of 'M' Division, had caused to be checked the lists of women notified to the police as missing during the period in question, twelve or eighteen months previously.

A coincidence emerged and because

detectives have frequently found that coincidences often lead to the discovery of important circumstantial evidence, Hatton's CID staff got a feeling they were on to something.

The coincidence was a missing woman named Dobkin, who had vanished some fifteen months before. Her husband had been a fire-watcher at 302, Upper Kennington Lane. He had looked after storage premises containing papers practically on the edge of the spot where the demolition workers had turned up the body. It was a pointer to a line of enquiry far too promising to be ignored.

Detective Inspector John Keeling, Hatton's second-in-command, obtained Dr Simpson's first findings and went to see Mrs Dobkin's sister (she had originally reported the disappearance to the police) in order to get a full description.

It was uncannily similar to the scientific reconstruction. The missing Mrs Rachel Dobkin had been 5ft 1in tall, with dark brown hair going gray. Her age had been forty-seven, and she had attended the London Hospital for a fibroid tumour of the uterus. Further enquiries began to turn up some very interesting facts.

The husband of the dead woman, Harry

Dobkin, was a bald, somewhat bull-like Jew of Russian birth[1] and just forty-nine years old. Before the war he worked as a ship's steward and cook, while, on shore, he managed to live by undertaking various jobs in the tailoring trade.

On 3 April 1941, a firm of solicitors engaged him as a fire-watcher to look after a small building belonging to them in which were stored quantities of papers and documents.

This building stood well back from the street in a yard containing the Vauxhall Baptist Church and its adjoining school, both places having been demolished by bombs. Two small houses fronting Upper Kennington Lane — between the Lane and the paper

---

[1] It may be of no possible sociological significance but of some interest that the origins of several people concerned in one way or another with notable British murder trials are remarkably varied; a casual handful picked haphazard from the headline names suggests the Island Race does not always lead: Florence Maybrick, American; Adelaide Bartlett, French; H. H. Crippen, American; George Chapman, Russian; Eugéne Marie Chantrelle, French; Buck Ruxton, Parsee; Jean Pierre Vaquier, French; Alma Rattenbury, Canadian; Oscar Slater, German, etc.

store — had also been bombed and were empty.

It was Dobkin's job to patrol round the paper store a prescribed number of times during the night in between which activities he made himself comfortable in a chair in one of the two small bombed houses. It would have been a pleasant life for a reflective man though, for certainty, Dobkin must have preferred to keep his mind strictly on the unforgiving minute and let the past bury itself.

A fortnight after his duties began, and, it was of interest to note, only very shortly after Mrs Dobkin's disappearance, there was a fire in the cellar under the site of the ruined church vestry. The fire brigade quickly put out the blaze, largely consisting of burning straw from a mattress lying within yards of the slab where later the scorched skeleton was to be found.

Dobkin at the time showed some agitation and made an odd, and uncalled-for, observation to a police constable that: 'I didn't do it.' The fire took place three days after Mrs Dobkin's sister reported the disappearance.

Police records revealed that as soon as news of the woman being missing was received, the husband was interviewed because, as I have mentioned before, police officers are inclined to go and talk lengthily to the husband when his wife vanishes — this is based on a simple, strictly sensible rule; frequently it pays dividends.

In this case Harry Dobkin made a statement which mentioned he had married a Rachel Dubinsky in 1920 at Bethnal Green Synagogue, a union that had failed from the beginning. A maintenance order for £1 weekly had been made against him a few months after the marriage, not that Mrs Dobkin ever succeeded in getting the stipulated amount from him. Becoming seriously in arrears over the payment landed Dobkin in jail for a brief term.

On 11 April 1941, Mrs Dobkin told her sister she was meeting her husband, apparently to try and coax some of the money due to her; as usual it was well behind. After lunch she set out and was seen in early evening by a waitress at a Dalston café having tea with Dobkin. That was the last of her so far as the world knew, though Dobkin was to swear he saw her off in an east-bound bus.

The following day her handbag, containing among other things an identity card and ration book, was found in a Guildford post office but never claimed. At five o'clock that afternoon Polly Dubinsky, the sister, gave information to the London police that Mrs

Dobkin was missing. She bluntly accused the husband, who had physically attacked his wife in the past, of being the responsible party.

In the resulting police investigation it was suspected that Dobkin must have started the fire in the church himself. Searches were made there without any result, though detectives were within inches of the concealing flagstone; apropos, a trench — 6ft by 1½ft — recently dug *was* found under the main church floor but there was no body in it.

Nothing ever came of this or of photographs published in the newspapers and gradually, through the enormous pressure of wartime work, the matter was dropped. Dobkin remained at his fire-watching job until May 1942, when his employers removed their documents and no longer required his services.

Having been a sort of custodian of the secret grave for all those months, Dobkin probably left his situation with some relief. It must have been galling for him to be told that within two months of quitting the post, demolition workers had retrieved the body and the problem of *Mrs Dobkin* had returned to the inquisitive world.

★ ★ ★

Dr Keith Simpson had already formed the private opinion that Dobkin must have murdered his wife by strangling in order to rid himself of an incubus, concealing the remains after mutilating the body and trying to destroy it by fire. The missing parts, never found, could easily have been disposed of in the Thames or in some similar way. But this was far from being a sound basis for a murder charge: identity had first to be transformed from a high probability into a complete certainty.

A technique was tried which Professor John Glaister and his colleagues initiated in the Ruxton murder case. The police had got hold of a portrait of Mrs Dobkin. It was enlarged for Dr Simpson to life size and a life size photograph of the jawless skull was taken. Superimposition of one on the other showed they corresponded exactly, the bony facial architecture forming a perfect foundation for the features in the portrait, the eye shape, set and angle aligning with the eye orifices in the skull and so on.

This was still by no means final. The next thing was the all-important dental data. Mrs Dobkin's dentist, on being found, supplied valuable evidence. This gentleman, Barnett A. Kopkin of North London, produced his dental treatment record card concerning this patient and was able to draw a diagram of Mrs Dobkin's upper jaw as he had last seen it together with fillings he had made.

The treatment given to the teeth in the skull was Kopkin's and later, seeing the actual teeth and their fillings, he immediately identified his work. He also stated that in extracting two teeth on the left side of the upper jaw in 1941, residual roots had been left, a not unusual occurrence. Sir William Kelsey Fry, a leading Guy's dental surgeon, made X-ray films of the skull and revealed those same roots. Identity was no longer in doubt.

Lastly, there was the question of how Mrs Dobkin had met her death.

The sprinkling of slaked lime on the body (the action of a layman in the belief that such lime destroys[1]) had preserved certain tissues round the neck. The hyoid and thyroid cartilages of the voice box were thus preserved, showing, on microscopical examination, clear traces of dried bruising. The

---

[1] From the wild inaccuracy laid down by a medical witness at the Manning trial in 1849 (and the belief existed earlier) that lime destroyed bodies, murderer after murderer has shown a pathetic devotion to lime as a decomposition agent, using it recklessly and time and again causing the victim's corpse to be properly *preserved* for subsequent investigations.

upper horn of the right wing of the voice box was fractured, this part of the bone being driven inwards towards the windpipe, and since the bruising surrounding the bone could only occur in life, Dr Simpson's view was that death resulted from manual strangulation, the only likely cause of such a fracture.

There was also found a blood-clot on the back of the head indicating heavy bruising which could have been inflicted by a backwards fall or the result of the head being dashed more than once against the ground by the violence of the strangler.

It was not a comfortable thought, the processes of that grim murder, the stripping of the tissues, the partial dismemberment and disposal of material, all to hide identity. The murderer's tenacity must have been remarkable, backed by a sort of malignant determination to destroy.

Not only is it hard work for the unskilled to hack up a dead body, but to remove tissue requires a steel-strong nerve, and an absolute lack of pity. As a practising crime novelist, I know only too well how glibly dismemberment can be written about, and how fictional licence can excuse or strengthen the criminal. In real life it is subject to a hundred hazards, quite apart from the physical repulsion felt by the ordinary person who undertakes such a deed.

At last Dr Simpson was satisfied, as far as any scientist ever can be satisfied, with his work that he had properly identified Mrs Rachel Dobkin after three months' steady probing into the mystery. He had given all his results to the police and in October Divisional Detective Inspector Hatton moved. Harry Dobkin was arrested and charged with the murder of his wife.

The Press, quite unaware of this impressive drama of detection going on behind the scenes, awoke to the case with much excitement by the time Dobkin appeared in Lambeth court for the preliminary hearing. Any time lost was made up by an elaborate coverage achieved against the vaster claims of war: as always one locally slaughtered female body was worth, in news value, a thousand dead soldiers overseas.

* * *

The trial at the Central Criminal Court took place before Mr Justice Wrottesley on 17 November 1942. It contained little drama and an enormous amount of detail.

112

Harry Dobkin was an uneasy captive in the dock. He seemed to glare a great deal at various people concerned with the prosecution side, and frowned heavily at times with the concentration of an empty mind. He was extremely fortunate in having his defence in the capable hands of Mr F. H. Lawton, a youthful barrister who was so highly regarded by the accused's solicitors that they did not brief a K C to lead him even though he had never before handled the defence in a trial for murder.

Dr Simpson was the last witness on the second day of the trial; he was taken carefully through his evidence by Mr L. A. (later Mr Justice) Byrne, for the Prosecution. To reproduce a part of the court examination is to show how every point was elaborated. The book frequently referred to was a volume of photographs, containing notes, for the enlightenment of the court, every photograph having been taken and prepared for the support of Dr Simpson's findings by Miss Newman, in charge of the Photographic Department at Guy's Hospital.

Mr Byrne: As to the identification of the body, I want to deal with that. You told us first of all you were able to determine the sex. That was comparatively simple, was it not?

A. Yes.

Q. Then did you determine how tall the woman had been?

A. Yes.

Q. How did you arrive at that?

A. I did it by two methods, the first by reconstructing as far as was possible the body as shown in Plate 2 and making due allowance for the missing parts, the joints at the knee and for the flesh and the feet, and by those means I estimated the stature to be 59¼ inches — that is to say, three-quarters of an inch short of five feet. I estimated the height to be about five feet and a quarter of an inch to five feet and three quarters of an inch.

Dr Simpson went on to explain his tables in the book which showed how he had arrived at the height estimates:

. . . I did this by two methods: by using the Pearson's formulae I estimated the height to be five foot and half an inch to five foot one inch, using the left humerus, the left upper-arm-bone, and by using the Rollet's tables, which are not so accurate in my view, I estimated the height to be four foot ten and a half inches to four foot ten inches. The mean of those estimations from both methods give a height estimation of about five foot and half an inch.

The question of the superimposition of the photographs on the dead woman's skull was explained in Dr Simpson's answer:

. . . The general contour of the skull was the same, allowing for scalp thickness; the contour of the cheeks, allowing for flesh, was the same; the position and shape of the upper jaw fitted the photograph well, was the same; the position, the height, and the width of the nose space were the same, and fitted perfectly.

On the following day the examination was resumed. Dr Simpson taken detail by detail through his findings, while the prosecution tested every fact and, indeed, re-tested it, so there could not be the slightest possible doubt.

In the minds of the listeners it was clear how the medico-legal case proved contentions offered by Dr Simpson, but in spite of it, Mr Lawton made a brave showing for the defence.

He went through the facts with the same care as Mr Byrne but sought to disprove them or find a weakness in Dr Simpson's conclusions. The superimposed photograph received a great deal of attention, pointed by Mr Lawton's remark that:

Is not the difficulty exaggerated in this way, that when taking a photograph one is obviously taking something in two dimensions, but when you are taking a photograph of a skull you are taking a photograph of something in three dimensions, and does not that tend to lead to inaccuracy in the two photographs?

A. That is one of the objections. That is a difficulty we had in this case; we had no measured portrait or anything by which we could measure the portrait precisely.

Q. And in particular when dealing with the photograph of a skull which in its three dimensions . . .

Mr Justice Wrottesley: I want to make sure that I follow that. When you say 'no means of measuring the portrait', that means you have no means of reducing the portrait to three dimensions?

116

A. No, it means that we do not know the precise width of the head and the height of the head in life from a portrait; we have nothing, as was so in the Ruxton case, by which the portrait could be measured.

Mr Lawton then made use of references to *Gray's Anatomy*, the standard medical work on the subject. He asked Dr Simpson:

Q. See if you can follow this passage: 'In comparing the shape of one skull with that of another it is necessary to adopt some definite position in which the skulls should be placed during the process of examination.' Obviously, they have both got to be placed in exactly the same position, have they not?
A. Yes.
Q. In this case you have not got a skull, but a photograph, and you cannot be certain, can you, that you had them in the identical positions?
A. The answer to that is that it was possible to move the skull so as to place it in the same position as the photograph.
Q. And in the same plane?
A. That is in the same position.

Q. Not quite, is it? You could have it in the same horizontal position, but not necessarily in the same plane.

A. This was in the same vertical and the same horizontal position.

With item after item concerning the skull discussed, and not to the advantage of the defence, the cross-examination moved on to a check on the structure of the voice box and the question of manual strangulation. It was also the defence's last effort to try and discover holes in the expert findings.

It was established that Dr Simpson found the whole of the voice box in connection with the body.

Q. By voice box do you just mean the thyroid or the two bones that go top and bottom of the thyroid?

A. I mean the hyoid, which is the upper bone shown in this photograph on which the tongue is placed, and also the two wings shown below of the thyroid. Those two together compose the voice box.

Mr Justice Wrottesley: Those three together?

A. Yes; I am taking those two below as one; those three together, yes.

118

Mr Lawton: In addition to those three bones, the hyoid and the two branches of the thyroid, there are one or two tiny bones, besides, are there not?

A. Yes, there may be.

Q. Many tiny bones besides?

A. There may be, yes.

Q. In particular there are two rather important tiny bones called the arytenoids?

A. There may be.

Q. There are, are there not?

A. There may be; they are not always bony.

Q. If they are not bony, they are in the nature of cartilages, are they not?

A. Yes.

Q. In fact, I am right in saying, am I not, that it is not until late in life that those bones, the hyoid and the thyroid, become bony at all?

A. About in middle life.

Q. Did you find the arytenoid cartilages?

A. Yes.

Q. And just above the horns of the thyroid there are two tiny cartilages known as the triticia, or something like that?

A. Yes.

Q. Did you find those?

A. Yes.

Q. I want you to assume that this situation arises: somebody standing in the road, or on a piece of waste ground, with a lot of rubble about, parts of bricks, and so on, being thrown violently forward by blast from a high explosive bomb, and in falling catching the voice box on a kerb or a piece of brick or masonry, or something of that sort. Is not it possible — I do not put it any higher than that — that a fall under those circumstances might break the cornu of the right thyroid?

A. I have seen injuries under those circumstances on many occasions, and the injuries have never been confined to a fracture of the cornu, as is present here.

Q. That may be, but have you seen injuries under those circumstances which have in fact broken a wing of the thyroid?

A. Yes, but not broken the cornu; broken the thyroid wing, yes. That is not what I described here.

Q. No, I know that, Doctor. I confused the two. Have you seen injuries in the street which have broken a wing of the thyroid and a horn of the thyroid?

A. I have seen both broken together.

Mr Justice Wrottesley: The broken wing being, of course, the lower part?

A. Yes; I have seen the whole thyroid crushed, with both cornu and both wings crushed.

Q. Is your evidence 'I have seen such injuries as are described by the throat hitting something'?

A. Yes.

Q. But they never occurred as here, that the thyroid was broken?

A. Yes. It is that which, in my view, is so significant.

Mr Lawton: Do you say it is impossible that a fall of the type I have described to you would break only the cornu of the thyroid?

A. I say that in fifteen years I have personally examined over 11,000 cases, and I have never seen this injury except in manual strangulation.

The defence had worked superbly against heavy odds. 'Mr Lawton,' one commentator rightly said, 'did everything except the impossible' which was to get his client free. The patient medical evidence was too careful and too precise to be argued away.

Dobkin was put in the witness box. If the

case against him was strong before he got there, the task was made much easier for the prosecution when Dobkin was to show himself a worse witness than anybody would have believed — it is ironic to think that the Criminal Evidence Act was meant as a privilege, and has often turned out to be the cause of many accused being convicted who, but for their showing in the box, might have got away with it.

Dobkin's eyes seemed to move sharply from point to point while his broad nostrils dilated continually during his destructive cross-examination by Mr Byrne. Most of the good work put in by pertinacious Mr Lawton was destroyed through Dobkin's reactions to certain questions.

In the end he was a sorry picture of panic and fear — I have seldom seen quite so grim a portrayal of a man betraying absolute guilt by a sort of gradual disintegration in which the shrivelled little soul was finally stripped bare of all pretence.

The steady hammering of the circumstantial evidence and Dr Simpson's work bore Dobkin down at every turn until he was accusing all the prosecution's witnesses of lying.

At some trials there always remains a feeling of doubt in the minds of certain of the expert spectators but Dobkin's prosecution was notable for the steady piling of fact on fact until the resulting edifice was as solid as the skills of science and detection could make it; the conclusions could not be gainsaid. There never was any question of Dobkin's guilt, and his protestations of innocence were futile. The defence tried to show the head bruising might have been a result of a fall by Mrs Dobkin after a bomb blast, and that, as a last surmise, the horn fracture was caused by a 'tiny bomb splinter passing into the neck from the rear and getting into the throat'. Dr Simpson thought this possible, but accepted it only as a remote chance. Granting such an event, there still remained the ancillary medical evidence, damning in itself.

For some there was the thought that perhaps, for all his brutality, Dobkin might not have premeditated his crime, that it was the result of overwhelming rage. Though he did what he did to get rid of the body, and he was a large man and she a small woman, it still might have been manslaughter. Yet, as he admitted nothing and flatly denied everything, the verdict of guilty was reached by the jury after only twenty minutes of consideration. It was by no means unexpected except, it would seem, by Dobkin. His features changed from white to red and back again, and he made a brief, rambling protest signifying nothing.

For Dr Keith Simpson, whose medical work had made the case into a modern classic,[1] there was to be one more meeting with Harry Dobkin.

It was on a foggy morning at Wandsworth Prison when, with the coroner and police officials, he made the customary post-mortem always held on the body of a hanged person. It is said that Dobkin looked peaceful.

What Dr Simpson thought at the completion of this full circle cannot be guessed, but at least he had the knowledge given to few men that his own reconstruction from poor fragments of a dead and dismembered woman had given her back an identity, with the result her murderer was caught and hanged, a just and rightful conclusion with which no fair man can possibly quarrel.

---

[1] The case has come to be quoted and written of in the standard textbooks on medico-legal subjects, as a classic example of the rewards of patient application of simple principles in identity reconstruction — comparing with, even exceeding in detail, the cases of Dr Parkman and Dr Ruxton. It happened also that it contained enough colour to achieve a place in the literature of crime detection.

THE JIGSAW MURDER CASE

(Dr Buck Ruxton, UK 1935)

Jonathan Goodman

The problem facing investigators in the gruesome Ruxton case was how to identify the human remains which had been wrapped in a newspaper like so much butcher's offal and thrown into a Scottish stream. Two heads were found, but the killer had been at pains to mutilate all the recognizable features: in one, the eyes had been removed, in the other, not just the eyes but the nose, lips and ears. The police believed they knew the identity of the two victims, and brought in two experts to help them prove it. Their brief, unprecedented in medico-legal history at the time, was to show conclusively that the remains were those of two women who had gone missing from home 100 miles away in Lancaster. The great forensic achievement was to show the astonished jury at Ruxton's trial life-sized photographs of the women in *life and pictures of the skulls found in Scotland. Superimposed one on top of the other, they fitted exactly. The tale is told by Britain's leading crime historian, Jonathan Goodman (b.1931). After a successful career in theatre and television production, in 1969 he published his classic re-examination of the Wallace murder case, the first of a series of true-crime books which established him as the pre-eminent investigator of past crimes. He has also written crime novels, verse, plays, television scripts, short stories and articles. Jonathan Goodman has most recently written and presented the Discovery Channel's series on historical crime,* Tales from the Black Museum.

If you are old enough to remember the first croonings of a romantic song, *Red Sails in the Sunset* — which, had there been such a thing as a pop chart in the mid-1930s, would have been top of it for a good many weeks — you may also recall an illicit version of the lyric which went like this:

> Red stains on the carpet,
> Red stains on your knife,
> Oh, Dr Buck Ruxton, you cut up your wife;
> The nursemaid, she saw you, and threatened to tell —

So, Dr Buck Ruxton, you killed her as well.

The fact that this anonymous rhyme was recited and sung on innumerable occasions gives an idea of the interest and excitement caused by a double murder in a small northern county town.

★   ★   ★

So far as public awareness is concerned, the case began on the bright but chilly afternoon of Sunday, 29 September 1935, when Susan Johnson, a young Edinburgh woman holidaying with her brother at Moffatt, a picturesque village thirty-five or so miles across the Scottish border from Carlisle, took a stroll to the bridge over Gardenholme Linn, a stream running into the River Annan.

Glancing over the rough stone parapet, she saw . . .

No, it couldn't possibly be.

She looked again. Her heart was thumping by now.

The second look convinced her that she was staring at a human arm, protruding from some wrapping at the side of the ravine.

Susan Johnson rushed back to the hotel. When she told her brother Alfred why she was in such a state, he asked the landlord to give her some medicinal whisky, then raced to the bridge. Clambering down the heather-strewn embankment, he saw not only an arm just above the waterline, some ten yards from the bridge, but an oddly-shaped bundle wrapped in bed-sheeting and newspaper.

He timorously pulled apart the wrapping and saw that the parcel contained chunks of flesh and bone.

Deciding that he had seen enough — more than enough — Alfred went in search of the village policeman and told him how the beauty of Gardenholme Linn had been marred.

After confirming that this was no false alarm, Constable James Fairweather telephoned the headquarters of the Dumfriesshire Constabulary, then went back to the bridge. And waited.

Not for long. Dumfries is no more than twenty miles from Moffatt, and Sergeant Robert Sloan rarely needed to slow down on the gently curving road that Sunday afternoon.

One wonders what went through his mind as he drove. Did he perhaps think about the Brighton Trunk crimes that had caused such a stir the year before? Did he fear that something similar — parcelled remains rather than bodies as luggage — would create as much work, as many problems, for himself and his colleagues?

He parked near the bridge, and had a few words with Constable Fairweather and Alfred Johnson; then treading carefully so as not to disturb the ground, he lowered himself down the side of the gully.

Within a few minutes, he had observed four parcels. After an hour, he had carefully parted the paper and sheeting and made a rough inventory of the respective contents, which included parts of legs, hands (with the tips of fingers and thumbs lopped off), thigh-bones, miscellaneous pieces of flesh, the chest portion of a human trunk, and two heads, hideously mutilated so as to be unrecognizable.

By the time Sloan had completed his notes and marked the positions of the parcels, other policemen had arrived from Dumfries. It was starting to get dark. Constable Fairweather unlocked the diminutive mortuary in Moffatt Cemetery, and the parcels were transported there.

During the next few days, forensic experts from Edinburgh and Glasgow visited the mortuary and made preliminary examinations of the decomposing, maggoty remains. One of the experts was John Glaister, who had been appointed Professor of Forensic Medicine at the University of Glasgow four years before, following the retirement of his famous father.

Then the 'bits and pieces,' as John Glaister referred to the remains, were taken to the anatomy department at Edinburgh University. Between the time of their arrival there and 4 November, they were augmented by the contents of other parcels found by the police and the public close to Gardenholme Linn and along the River Annan. The parcel farthest removed from those that had started the investigation was discovered at Johnson Bridge, on the main Edinburgh-Carlisle road, nine miles from Moffatt.

The malformed, 'Cyclops' eye of an animal was found among the remains. It was better preserved than the human flesh and tissues, suggesting that it had been immersed in formaldehyde, perhaps by someone interested in ophthalmology.

While the pathologists, an anatomist and a dentist tried to solve the two 'jigsaw puzzles', and to find distinguishing marks to assist in identifying the victims, the police made inquiries about persons reported missing before 19 September, when there had been torrential rain in the area around Moffatt, filling streams and rivers; it seemed clear that the parcels had been left behind on the banks as the level of the water had fallen.

The police had one apparently important clue. A piece of newspaper that had helped to wrap one of the packages was recognized as being part of the *Sunday Graphic* of 15 September 1935: part of a special 'slip' edition of 3,700 copies, carrying a report and pictures of the crowning of the Morecambe Carnival Queen, that had been distributed only around Morecambe and the nearby county town of Lancaster.

On the very same day that the Chief Constable of Dumfries got in touch with the Lancaster police, he happened to notice a report in the *Glasgow Daily Record*. Briefly tucked away on an inside page, the report referred to the disappearance, in mid-September, of Mary Jane Rogerson, the twenty-year-old nursemaid to the children of an Indian doctor named Buck Ruxton, who ministered to the sick at his home at 2 Dalton Square, Lancaster, 105 miles south of the bridge over Gardenholme Linn.

Struck by the Lancasterian coincidence, the Chief Constable initiated inquiries in that town. He soon learned that the disappearance of Mary Rogerson had been notified to the local police — also that there was a rumour that Dr Ruxton's wife had left him at about the time the nursemaid was last seen.

A detective was sent to get a detailed

description of the missing girl from her stepmother, who lived in Morecambe, and as a result of the visit two further pieces of information came to light.

The human remains found at and near Moffatt had been wrapped mainly in newspaper and bed-linen — but a blouse and a child's romper suit had also been used. When the blouse was shown to Mrs Rogerson, she at once recognized it, saying that she had bought it at a jumble sale and given it to Mary just before Christmas 1934; she had no doubt that it was the same blouse, for she had sewn a patch under one of the arms.

Mrs Rogerson told the police that, during the summer, her stepdaughter and two of the Ruxtons' three children had spent a fortnight in a guesthouse at Grange-over-Sands, and that the landlady had given Mary some secondhand clothes.

A detective visited the landlady, Mrs Edith Holme, who instantly identified the romper suit as one of the things she had given the nursemaid: her own child had outgrown the suit; before parting with it, she had put new elastic in the waistband, tying the ends in a knot of her invention.

So far, the control and conduct of the investigation had been emphatically Scottish;

but now, although the scientific work of piecing together the assortment of human remains continued in Edinburgh, overall responsibility for the case was passed to Captain Henry Vann, the Chief Constable of Lancaster.

Captain Vann and his subordinates already knew quite a lot about Dr Buck Ruxton — and in a few days, without having to put themselves out to any great extent, they learned much more.

When Ruxton was born in Bombay, in 1899, he was called Bukhtar Rustomji Ratanji Hakim, or Buck Hakim for short, but some thirty years later he anglicised his name by deed poll.

He was touchy about being referred to simply as an Indian, and would insist on the more specific designation of Parsee, pointing out that he was a descendant of the Zoroastrians who migrated from Persia to India in the eighth century.

He held three medical degrees, two from the University of Bombay and one (MB) from the University of London.

After gaining the first of those degrees, he served for about three years in the Indian Medical Corps and then travelled to Britain, where he lived first of all in London, working as a locum while pursuing

133

his studies, and then in Edinburgh, preparing for the examinations for Fellowship of the Royal College of Surgeons of that city.

His failure in that examination may have been due, at least in part, to the fact that his dedication to his studies was diminished by his infatuation for Isabella Van Ess, a woman two years younger than himself who, following her estrangement from her Dutch husband, was working as a waitress in a restaurant in Princes Street, Edinburgh.

Sharp-nosed, wide-mouthed, and with legs that did not narrow towards the ankles, Isabella was far less lovely than her name; but still, Ruxton was smitten from the moment she first took an order from him for tea and scones.

Presumably because he decided that Isabella would consider him more dashing if she thought he was an army officer, decently reticent about his many decorations for gallantry, he led her to believe that he was Captain Hakim.

He returned to London at the beginning of 1928, and Isabella joined him soon afterwards. Though she was now divorced, and though between 1929 and 1933 she gave birth to three children, she never married Ruxton.

In 1930, Dr and 'Mrs' Ruxton, with their first child, Elizabeth, moved to 2 Dalton Square, a grey-stone terrace house of three storeys and a basement that stood next to a picture palace in the centre of Lancaster. Of the four rooms on the ground floor, two each side of a hall, Ruxton used three for his general medical practice, one as a waiting room, one for consultations, the third as a surgery; the fourth room, at the back, was a kitchen.

There were two living rooms and a dining room on the first floor, and at some time since the house had been built, towards the end of the nineteenth century, a bathroom had been squeezed in as a sort of addition to the first-floor landing. There was a master bedroom and three smaller ones on the top floor.

Ruxton soon had a large panel of patients. This was partly due to an insufficiency of doctors in the town, partly because his practice was very general indeed, including even dentistry and ophthalmology, and partly because he seemed invariably affable, worthy of the locals' descriptions of him as 'that nice, obliging, young foreign doctor'.

But Isabella did not consider him alto-gether nice. As the months, the years, went by, the couple quarrelled with increasing frequency and vehemence.

Sometimes the rows were over what Ruxton called 'Belle's temporary sillinesses'. Sometimes the cause was jealousy: Ruxton was particularly suspicious of a friend of Isabella's, a young man called Bobby Edmondson who worked in the solicitor's department at the town hall, just across the square from the doctor's house. And sometimes there was a sexual motive for the arguments, for both Ruxton and Isabella experienced enhanced pleasure from intimacy when it was part of 'making-up'.

By April 1935, Isabella was either tired of Ruxton's tantrums or terrified by his bad temper. As the result of a statement she made to a detective, Ruxton was invited to the police station. When he saw his 'wife' there, he (in the detective's words) 'flew into a violent passion and said, 'My wife has been unfaithful. I would be justified in murdering her'.'

The detective pacified Ruxton (or thought so), reassured Isabella (or believed that he had), and put the incident out of his mind — until a month or so later, when he was called to 2 Dalton Square, again to act as peace-maker.

It would have been better for Isabella — and for the young nursemaid, Mary Rogerson — if, instead of seeking help from the police, she had waited until Buck Ruxton was answering a housecall and then escaped to a place where he might not find her or could not harm her.

★   ★   ★

Following the press reports of the gruesome discoveries at Moffatt — and long before the police suspected Ruxton of murder — a good many people in Lancaster, including the doctor's several charwomen and some of his patients and neighbours, wondered whether there was a connection between what they had read in the papers and the disappearance of Mrs Ruxton and the nursemaid.

Both before and after the mutilated remains were found, Ruxton contended on various occasions and to various people that the two women had gone to Blackpool ... that they were taking a holiday in Scotland ... that the nursemaid was pregnant, so Isabella might have taken her away for an abortion ... that Isabella had gone off with a lover ... that she had returned to London.

When early newspaper accounts stated (wrongly, as it turned out) that some of the remains found at Moffatt were of a man, Ruxton was joyful. After giving one of the

137

charwomen a rest from her chores while he read aloud a report of the 'Ravine Murder,' he chortled, 'So you see, Mrs Oxley, it is a man and a woman — not our two,' then burst into helpless laughter at Mrs Oxley's response that she sincerely hoped not.

But within a week of that incident he was distinctly unhappy about what the papers were saying. He turned up at the police station at half-past nine on the night of Friday, 11 October, and, waving a copy of the *Daily Express* in one hand and furiously gesticulating with the other, screamed at the Chief Constable that such publicity was ruining his practice.

While Captain Vann tried to get a word in edgeways, Ruxton sat on the desk, perched his feet on a visitor's chair, and banged the back of it with his free hand.

Abruptly changing the subject — and crying now — Ruxton accused a man of being Isabella's lover, claimed that he had tapped telephone conversations between them, and implored Captain Vann to intercept the alleged lover's mail.

Then, reverting to the press, he asked the Chief Constable to issue a statement that the remains found in and around Moffatt were not those of Isabella and Mary Rogerson. Captain Vann was still uming and ahing about

138

that when the doctor stalked out.

Uming and ahing . . . ? Well, yes. If only because Ruxton's arrival had interrupted a discussion between Captain Vann and a senior detective as to whether the time was ripe to charge the doctor with double murder.

Ever since the responsibility for the investigation had been passed to Lancaster from Dumfriesshire, the Lancaster Borough Police Force had been just as busy as the scientists gathered in the anatomy department at Edinburgh University, piecing together the incomplete jigsaws of flesh and bone, and drawing conclusions from what they found — and could not find.

The police knew, among many other things, that on Saturday, 14 September, Mrs Ruxton had driven to Blackpool in the doctor's Hillman car, registration number CP 8415, to see the illuminations with her two sisters, and that she had started the return journey just before midnight. Though she was never seen alive again, the presence of the car in Lancaster the next day indicated that she had arrived home.

Some of the strongest evidence against Ruxton came from his charwomen. At half-past six on the morning of Sunday, 15 September, Mrs Agnes Oxley was getting ready to go to the doctor's house when

Ruxton drove up in his car and told her that she could have the day off as 'Mrs Ruxton and Mary have gone away on a holiday to Edinburgh'.

That afternoon, however, the doctor visited one of his patients, Mrs Mary Hampshire, and asked if she wanted to earn seven shillings and sixpence by scrubbing his staircase. He explained that he needed her help because Isabella was in Blackpool and Mary Rogerson in Edinburgh, and he had cut his hand badly in trying to open a tin of peaches for the children's breakfast. (He certainly had a severe wound on one of his fingers, and a subsequent remark to Mrs Hampshire that he had taken his children to stay with a dentist friend in Morecambe was true.)

When Mrs Hampshire arrived at 2 Dalton Square, she found that the place was far more messy and untidy than she had expected: the carpets had been taken from the stairs, which were scattered with straw; rolled-up carpets, stair-pads and a man's suit were lying in the waiting room, and in the back yard were other carpets, clothing and towels, all heavily stained with blood and showing signs that an attempt had been made to burn them.

Mrs Hampshire, a trusting soul, accepted the doctor's explanation that the carpets had been taken up because the house was to be decorated, and seems to have assumed that, though Ruxton did not look anaemic, the blood saturating the things in the yard had flowed from the cut on his finger.

She did not ask him to explain the straw protruding from beneath the doors to two of the bedrooms — or why those doors were locked and the keys removed.

Mrs Hampshire started tidying up, and, when her husband came to the house a few hours later, got him to lend a hand. Ruxton gave the couple a load of soiled carpets and clothing, but presumably Mrs Hampshire was paid more than the promised seven shillings and sixpence for her labours, not only on the Sunday but on subsequent days, on some of which she was assisted by the doctor's regular chars.

The police had much more evidence against Ruxton, including the testimony of a cyclist who on Tuesday, 17 September, had been knocked over by the doctor's car on a road leading to Moffatt; Ruxton had not stopped but was caught by a policeman, who noted that he was as jumpy as a flea.

But all this evidence might be insufficient to convict Buck Ruxton if the scientists in Edinburgh were unable to establish that the bits and pieces of flesh and bone on their laboratory tables were the remains of Isabella Ruxton and Mary Rogerson.

★ ★ ★

It was vital that the separated, mutilated remains found in Dumfriesshire be identified as those of the doctor's common-law wife and his children's nursemaid. Admittedly, by the time of the Ruxton case there can have been few judges who wholly accepted Lord Halsbury's contention that 'in the absence of evidence (that a body or part of a body has been found, which is proved to be that of the person alleged to have been killed) there is no onus upon the prisoner to account for the disappearance or non-production of the person.'

Only the year before, a man named Davidson had been convicted of the murder of his small son though no body had been found, the presumption being that the body was consumed in a fire on a garbage tip.

But a clever defence lawyer might confuse less clever members of a jury about the meaning of 'reasonable doubt' by speaking of ancient cases in which men had been hanged for the murder of people who had afterwards, like Mark Twain, complained of reports of their demise, and use any uncertainty concerning the fact of death to suggest uncertainty about the act of murder.

The team of experts at Edinburgh University not only used accepted methods but invented new techniques as they sorted out which of the remains belonged to one body, which to the other — as they then searched for clues that might, singly or in relation to others, give more reality to the incomplete bodies than the original designations of 'No 1' and 'No 2' — as they sought indications of the cause, or causes of death.

Probably for the first time, an anatomist had been brought into a murder investigation. This was James Couper Brash, professor of anatomy at the University of Edinburgh — a city that, a hundred or so years before, had become associated, through the activities of Burke and Hare, with the unlawful aspects of the science.

Brash was able to get an exact fit between some of the dismembered remains and, using anatomical formulae and X-rays, classified other parts as belonging to one body or the other.

After weeks of work, two partially reconstructed bodies lay side by side on tables in the laboratory. 'No 1' was less complete than 'No 2', but Brash had gauged the living stature of the bodies as, respectively, five feet and five feet and three inches.

There was ample evidence that both bodies were female. If — a very large 'if' at this stage — they were of the women from 2 Dalton Square Lancaster, then 'No 1' was Mary Rogerson and 'No 2' was Mrs Ruxton.

With help from an odontologist, Arthur Hutchinson, Brash estimated the age of 'No 1' as 20 (as was the nursemaid) and that of 'No 2' as being between 35 and 45 (Isabella Ruxton was 34).

Paradoxically, many of the mutilations of the remains assisted the pathologists in their search for evidence. The manner of dismemberment (without the use of a saw and with only slight damage to the separated parts), together with the fact that components that might have indicated cause of death had been removed, showed that the criminal was skilled in the use of surgical knives and that he had anatomical and medical knowledge.

The criminal had removed from both heads the eyes, ears, lips and nose — in all of which signs of asphyxia might be found — but so far as body 'No 2' was concerned, there remained several indications that death was due to asphyxia by throttling.

The most iterated example of 'negative evidence' comes from fiction — the dog that, as Sherlock Holmes noted, did not bark in the night. For a real-life example, it would be hard to better what the experts in the Ruxton investigation noted as being absent from the remains.

Virtually from the start, John Glaister and his colleagues supposed that the reason for many of the mutilations was to make identification more difficult, but it was not until the scientists knew some of the distinguishing features of the two missing women that they began to suspect answers to specific questions.

Perhaps the eyes of body 'No 1' had been taken out because Mary Rogerson had a cast in one eye. Had the skin been removed from the upper part of the right forearm because Mary had a conspicuous birthmark there? Were the soft tissues shaved from the right thumb because the nursemaid had a scar there?

And had the nose of body 'No 2' been cut off, and the teeth been extracted, because those were prominent features of Mrs Ruxton? Had the soft tissues of the legs been removed because Isabella's legs were the same thickness from the knees to the ankles? Were the toes lopped off because Isabella's were 'humped'?

So many of the sites of the excisions and mutilations corresponded with those of distinguishing features of the missing women that there seemed only one answer. Added to the evidence already gathered, the 'negative evidence' virtually proved that the bodies were those of Isabella Ruxton and Mary Rogerson.

But to make assurance double sure, James Brash did something that, so far as is known, had never been attempted in a criminal investigation. After obtaining photographs of the missing women, he arranged for the head and shoulders in each to be enlarged to life-size. He took immense care to ensure that the size of the enlargements was correct; for instance, a piece of jewellery worn by Mrs Ruxton in one of the photographs was located and measured to the nearest millimetre, so that the size could be used to establish the measurements of her head and features. The enlarged photographs were then superimposed on photographs, taken to the exact size, of the decapitated heads in the laboratory. The resulting 'double exposures' showed a remarkable correspondence.

On Saturday, 12 October, after the evidence assembled by the Scottish scientists had been added to that gathered by the police, Chief Constable Vann invited Buck Ruxton to his office.

The doctor arrived at 9.30 in the evening

and spent the next ten hours answering questions. Then he was charged with the murder of Mary Rogerson.

He looked flabbergasted. 'Most emphatically not,' he spluttered. 'Of course not. The farthest thing from my mind. What motive and why? What are you talking about?'

Following Ruxton's arrest (on 5 November he was further charged with the murder of Isabella), the investigators searched the house in Dalton Square for more indications of his guilt.

They found a good many, of which the most important, perhaps, was a sheet that had precisely the same peculiar fault in the selvedge as did pieces of a sheet that had been used as wrapping for the hideous bundles found at Moffatt.

By the start of the new year, the investigators believed that the case against Buck Ruxton was complete, watertight.

But then they learned something that worried them greatly: the doctor was to be defended at the trial by the velvet-voiced Norman Birkett, who was thought of by some people as 'the courtroom magician', by others as 'the murderer's best friend'.

If anyone could persuade the jury in the Ruxton case to return a nonsensical verdict, it was Birkett.

The trial started on Monday, 2 March 1936, at the old Manchester Assize Court in Great Ducie Street, with Mr Justice Singleton, a stickler for the niceties of courtroom behaviour, presiding.

J. C. Jackson, one of the best-known silks on the Northern circuit, led for the Crown, assisted by two barristers who would rise to high positions in government: one, a Socialist, was Hartley Shawcross, and the other, a Tory, inspired the couplet:

The closest thing to death in life
Is David Patrick Maxwell Fyfe.

Buck Ruxton's defender, the tall, bespectacled Norman Birkett, made few notes during the opening speech for the prosecution; but right from the start, Ruxton, sitting in the dock behind Birkett, scribbled messages to his counsel.

According to Mr Jackson's view of what had happened in the house in Dalton Square, Lancaster, after Mrs Ruxton's trip to see the Blackpool illuminations: 'When she went up to bed, a violent quarrel took place; Ruxton strangled his wife, and Mary Rogerson caught him in the act and had to die also.'

148

There was, of course, much more to Mr Jackson's speech than that; he dealt with every aspect of the case, occasionally in greater detail than some observers thought necessary, starting with the discovery of the human remains at Moffatt and concluding with the arrest of the Indian doctor.

The speech went on till late in the afternoon, leaving only enough time for four prosecution witnesses to be called that day. Though the evidence of those witnesses was formal — to do with plans, photographs and the like — Norman Birkett cross-examined each of them in some depth.

And during the following seven days of the trial, hardly any of the prosecution witnesses — over a hundred of them — left the court without having been questioned by Birkett. At times, when there was a flurry of requests by counsel for the production of exhibits, the well of the court looked like an untidy jumble sale, with bottles, jewellery, books and kitchenware scattered over piles of clothing, carpets and bed-linen.

Mrs Mary Hampshire, one of the several women who had laboured to make the doctor's house presentable after the disappearance of Mrs Ruxton and the nursemaid, fainted in the witness box. Perhaps the sight of some bloodstained carpets, given to her by the generous doctor but taken from her by the police and now exhibits, made her feel queasy. As she was being carried from the court, the doctor peered from the dock at his former patient and gave his professional opinion that she would be all right. When she returned, he made a what-did-I-tell-you? gesture, then started scribbling again.

The last of the Crown's witnesses were the Scottish scientists who had made medico-legal history by their reconstruction and scrutiny of the bodies. They had done their work so thoroughly that Birkett scored few, and then only minor, successes in cross-examination.

Before the last of the scientists was called, Birkett wrote a memorandum for Ruxton's solicitor to show his client. It ended:

'In my clear and very strong view, if Dr Ruxton desires to give evidence, we should confine our evidence to him, and exercise our right of the last word to the jury . . . Any other course, in my view, would be absolutely fatal.'

Ruxton agreed, and on the morning of the eighth day of the trial was escorted from the dock to be the sole witness in his own defence.

His solicitor had warned him that he must remain calm, listen carefully to each question, and restrict his answers to what had been asked, but the flashily handsome doctor soon forgot — or, believing that he knew best, ignored — the advice.

After asking a few 'tuning-up' questions, Birkett inquired about Ruxton's relations with Isabella — and was made most unhappy by the reply: 'If I may be permitted to put it in appropriate English, I can honestly say we were the kind of people who could not live with each other and could not live without each other.'

Not finished yet, Ruxton said something that his counsel didn't understand.

'You have added something else,' Birkett muttered irritably.

'Forgive me the interruption,' said Ruxton, 'but I just used the French proverb, 'Who loves most chastises most.' My mentality thinks in French, and I have to translate into English everything you are asking me.'

No doubt feeling that his task was hard enough without the imposition of a language barrier, Birkett from now on tried to leap in with a question as soon as Ruxton had delivered the first sentence of his answer to the previous one.

But Birkett was rarely fast enough, and

eventually snapped, 'Perhaps you will just deal only with the questions I put to you.'

No use: the words continued to tumble out, and every so often Ruxton burst into tears.

His answers to two successive questions are often quoted to exemplify how witnesses should not respond.

Birkett asked, 'It is suggested here by the Crown that on the morning of the Sunday after your wife had come back, you killed her?'

'That is an absolute and deliberate and fantastic story,' the doctor screamed, waving his arms about. 'You might just as well say the sun was rising in the west and setting in the east.'

Next question: 'It is suggested also by the Crown that, upon that morning, you killed Mary Rogerson?'

'That is absolute bunkum, with a capital B, if I may say it. Why should I kill my poor Mary?'

It may be that the jury never made up their minds about that — or about the motive for Isabella's murder — but after another couple of days, which included the cross-examination of Ruxton, the closing speeches, and the judge's summing-up, the jury returned a verdict of Guilty.

Asked if he had anything to say why

sentence of death should not be passed, Ruxton raised his right hand, the palm towards the judge, in what could have been a salute or a blessing, and uttered some flowery but irrelevant remarks. He made the same gesture as the judge spoke the final words of the death sentence, then bowed before being escorted from the dock.

Six weeks later, after the doctor's appeal was dismissed, something rather odd happened. In towns from one end of the country to the other, masses of people, few of them certifiably insane, signed petitions for a reprieve; in Lancaster alone, there were six thousand signatories.

But the Home Secretary had the good sense to ignore the petitions, and Ruxton was hanged at Strangeways Prison, Manchester, on the fine morning of Tuesday, 12 May.

The following Sunday, anyone who had signed a petition and was also a reader of the *News of the World* should have been a trifle embarrassed. There on the front page was a facsimile of a confession to the two murders that the good doctor had written the day after he was arrested.

A CASE OF 'HIDEOUS FEROCITY'

(Peter Griffiths, UK 1948)

Norman Lucas

Peter Griffiths, the killer of little June Devaney, was caught by his fingerprints. Griffiths had crept into a hospital ward in Blackburn where the child was sleeping and taken her from her cot. The child's body was found in the hospital grounds. She had been brutally raped. The murderer's fingerprints were found on a bottle by the child's cot. Three days after the killing, the baffled police took an unprecedented step. They decided to fingerprint the entire male population of Blackburn. Every one of the town's 35,000 homes was visited, and every man and boy aged sixteen or over asked for his prints. It was a long, laborious task, and early results were not encouraging. The breakthrough came after three months and more than 46,000 sets of prints. Peter Griffiths thought he'd slipped through the net because his name didn't appear on the local electoral roll. But he'd reckoned without the records of wartime ration books. After Griffiths' execution, the prints taken in the course of the inquiry were publicly burned. Norman Lucas (1920–98) was the Sunday Mirror's chief crime reporter. He exposed the Kray mob in London's East End and broke the story of the first child's body being uncovered by Lancashire police in the Moors murders of the 1960s. Norman Lucas's experiences enabled him to write seventeen books on crime, two of which were reprinted in seven languages including Czech and Japanese.

On the night of 14–15 May 1948, little June Anne Devaney was sleeping soundly in her cot in the babies' ward of Queen's Park Hospital, Blackburn, Lancashire. She had been suffering from pneumonia, but after ten days in hospital had been pronounced well enough to return to her parents, Mr and Mrs Albert Devaney, who lived in Princess Street, in the Waterfall district of the town.

It had been arranged that her aunt, Mrs Ann Whalley, would collect her the following day because Mrs Devaney, in addition to two other children at home, had had a new baby — born 5 May, the day June had been taken to hospital.

June, a big girl for her age — three years and eleven months although she looked about six years old — was very bright and intelligent. That evening she had been chattering happily to the nurses, and to her new black doll, about going home to Mummy and Daddy and seeing the new baby.

She was the eldest of the six children in the ward and the only one who could talk.

At 11.30 that night Nurse Gwendoline Humphreys took over duty in the babies' ward and the adjoining toddlers' ward, in which there were several more older children. She looked round both wards and the sun room and a side room, then went into the kitchen to start preparations for the children's breakfast. While she was seeing to the porridge she heard a child crying and found it was Michael Tattersall, a baby in the next bed to June Devaney. In her rubber-soled shoes she tiptoed to Michael's side and remained with him for about twenty minutes. She noticed that little June was fast asleep, and returned to the kitchen. Just before 12.30 she thought she heard a girl's voice from the direction of the porch door and went to investigate. She looked out into the moonlit grounds but could not see anyone, then a little girl in the toddlers' ward began to cry and she spent about fifteen minutes with her.

At 1.15 a.m. Nurse Humphreys returned to the babies' ward and immediately noticed that June Devaney's cot was empty. She looked around the ward and in the toilet, but there was no sign of the child. The nurse also noticed that a Winchester bottle of sterile water, which had been on a trolley in the ward, was lying beneath June's cot. Then, to her horror, she saw what looked like the prints of large bare feet running the whole length of the highly polished ward floor and more footprints beside June's cot. Nurse Humphreys raised the alarm and the police were called.

June's father, a thirty-three-year-old foundry worker, joined in a search of the hospital and grounds, and he was with the police when at 3.15 a.m. they found the body of his little girl. She was lying in the grass near a stone wall encircling the hospital grounds and it was plain that she had been raped and battered to death.

Within an hour of their gruesome discovery the local police had called in the country police and the country police sought the aid of Scotland Yard, so that by noon of the day of the murder the Chief Constable of Blackburn, Mr C. G. Looms, was conferring with Detective Chief Inspector Robert McCartney, of the Lancashire Constabulary, and Detective Superintendent Jack ('Charlie Artful') Capstick, of the Yard's Murder Squad.

Only the previous evening Capstick had arrived back in London after two months of intensive inquiries into the murder of Jack Quentin Smith, an eleven-year-old schoolboy who had been found stabbed and battered to death in Farnworth — barely thirteen miles from Blackburn. The police had a description of his killer — thin, tall and youngish, with deep-set eyes and a pimply face — given by another boy, David Lee, who had been attacked at the same time but had managed to escape. All possible leads to the boy's killer had proved abortive and Capstick returned to London for a conference at the Yard.

He was more than usually concerned at the failure to capture little Jack Smith's murderer because four years earlier a six-year-old girl, Sheila Fox, had disappeared on her way home from school in Farnworth, and within less than two years another child in the same town — nine-year-old Patricia McKeon — had been attacked near her home.

Not unnaturally, parents in that area of Lancashire were beginning to be really frightened and the murder of baby June added to the rapidly growing rumours that a 'moon maniac' was at large.

It was four o'clock in the morning of 15 May when Jack Capstick, after only an hour or two in bed, was woken by the phone and told by Chief Constable Looms about the murder of June Devaney. By 6.20 a.m. Capstick and the late Detective Sergeant John Stoneham were on their way back to Lancashire, arriving in Blackburn by lunch-time.

In the meantime Detective Inspector Colin Campbell, chief of the Lancashire County Constabulary Fingerprint Bureau, had found an enormous number of confused finger-prints on the Winchester bottle which had been found under June's bed, and among them were seemingly fresh thumb, index finger and palm prints. The footprints on the ward floor were photographed and were shown to have been made not by naked feet, but by large feet enclosed in socks. The pattern of the weave was clearly revealed and a few tiny fibres of wool from the socks were found adhering to the wax polish on the floor.

The prints on the bottle showed that the killer had big hands; those on the floor indicated large feet; the fact that there were no hand prints on June's cot meant that the child had probably been removed without the side of the cot being lowered — in other words the police had a picture of a killer who

159

was tall enough to have leaned over the rail and lifted her out of her bed. They knew they were looking for a man with big hands and feet who was probably familiar with the layout of the hospital building and grounds.

Everyone who might legitimately have handled the Winchester bottle was finger-printed — nurses, doctors, relief staff, patients' visitors, ambulance drivers, electricians who had worked in the ward, and tradesmen delivering goods. In three days 642 sets of prints were taken from people who might have handled the bottle in the preceding two years. This check eliminated many prints but still left the fresh prints believed to have been made by the killer.

Because the police were convinced that he was a local man familiar with the hospital routine, the finger-printing was extended to all men who had been patients in the last two years, all male visitors to the hospital, ex-members of the staff, husbands and boyfriends of nurses — bringing the total prints to more than 2,000. But still the vital prints remained unidentified.

Then Detective Superintendent Capstick put forward an idea which was at first regarded as impractical and impossible to implement — to fingerprint every male over the age of fourteen in the whole town of

Blackburn. There had never been a mass fingerprinting of a town's population before and it was doubted if the people would co-operate. The Mayor gave the lead by volunteering to be first and the response of the town was very wholehearted. An undertaking was given that all fingerprints obtained in this great check-up would be destroyed when their purpose had been served, and the 50,000 prints were in fact ceremonially destroyed at a later date.

Every one of the 35,000 houses in the borough was visited, but the check had necessarily to go further afield because some men who had been in Blackburn on the night of the murder had moved. Some had been visitors, others seamen who had rejoined their ships or members of the armed forces who had returned to their units. Eventually prints were forwarded to Blackburn from places as far afield as South America, Sweden, Hong Kong, South Africa and Canada.

But still, none matched the vital prints on the Winchester bottle.

In the meantime the usual red herrings had been drawn across the path of detection. Two parties of nurses returning to the hospital on the night of the murder said they had been accosted by a man near the gates and had experienced difficulty in evading him while other nurses reported seeing a 'Peeping Tom' peering into a bedroom window of the nurses' home. When this man was traced he was found to be the husband of a woman in the maternity ward. He was quickly eliminated from the inquiry.

A youth then came forward and confessed to the murder, and was found to be the same lad who had confessed to the murder of Jack Quentin Smith a few weeks previously. It was proved conclusively that he could have had nothing to do with either of the killings.

At this point in the inquiry the police had their first lucky break.

Food was still rationed in that post-war year of 1948 and in August a new issue of books was due. Inspector Bill Barton, of the Blackburn police, had the bright idea of checking the names on the enormous pile of fingerprints with the list of new ration books to be issued — and it was found that 200 men and youths had either deliberately or involuntarily slipped through the net.

So the final search began. Among the missing 200 was a twenty-two-year-old ex-Guardsman named Peter Griffiths living in Birley Street, Blackburn, who was seen by Police Constable Joseph Calvert on 11 August. Griffiths, then working as a flour mill packer, had somehow evaded the fingerprinting team when they had called at his house during the first big check, but raised no objection to having his prints taken when the second call was made.

The prints were sent for examination by the experts — and were found to match exactly those on the Winchester bottle.

At nine-thirty in the evening of 13 August Jack Capstick and Inspector Barton stopped Griffiths as he left 31 Birley Street, where he lived with his father Peter Griffiths senior, his mother, Mrs Elizabeth Griffiths, and his half-brother, James Brennan.

Told that he was to be arrested for the murder of June Devaney, he said: 'What is it to do with me? I have never been near the place.' Later he asked: 'Is it my fingerprints why you came to see me?' He was told that it was.

He then said, 'Well if they are my fingerprints on the bottle, I will tell you all about it'. He made a statement in which he said that on the night of the murder he intended to spend a quiet evening on his own.

He had five pints of bitter at the Dun Horse public house, then went on to Yates Wine Lodge where he had two glasses of Guinness and two double rums. He returned to the Dun Horse and had about six more pints of bitter, leaving at closing time. In Jubilee Street a man in a car asked him if he would like a 'spin' and took him to the front of Queen's Park Hospital.

'The next thing I remember was being outside the ward where there was some children,' he said. 'I left my shoes outside a door . . . it opened to my touch and I went in. I heard a nurse humming and banging things . . . so I came out again and waited a few minutes. Then I went back in again. I picked up a biggish bottle off a shelf . . . I overbalanced and fell against a bed. I remember a child woke up and started to cry and I hushed her. I picked the girl up out of the cot and took her outside. She put her arms round my neck and I walked with her down the hospital field. I put her down on the grass. She started crying again and I tried to stop her, but she wouldn't do like . . . I just lost my temper and you know what happened. I banged her head against the wall. I then went back to the veranda outside the ward and put my shoes on. I went back to where the child was, I just glanced at her but did not go right up to her but went straight on down the field.'

Griffiths added that when he got home he slept on a couch downstairs. The following day he had his breakfast, went for a walk and then to a cinema and later returned home to tea.

'I looked at the papers and read about the murder,' he said. 'It didn't shake me so I just carried on normally after that. That is all I can say and I'm sorry for both parents' sake and I hope I get what I deserve.'

On the day following Griffiths' arrest the police recovered from a local pawnbroker the suit the accused man had worn on the night of the murder. Bloodstains on the jacket and trousers were found to be of Group 'A' — the same as the dead child's blood group — and fibres from the suit matched some found on her nightdress and body. Tests on a pair of Griffiths' socks showed that the colour, method of weave and number of twists to the inch tallied with the socks worn by the murderer as he walked through the ward. His footprints, too, matched those on the waxed floor.

A Miss Rene Edge told the police that on Sunday, 16 May — the day after the murder — she had gone for a walk with Griffiths and he had shown her a bloodstained Soldiers' Song Book. She asked how the blood had got there and he told her he cut his hand during a fight when he was in the Army.

Griffiths had been 'walking out' with Miss

Edge, a quiet, religious girl, for some time, but she did not approve of his drinking and in April that year had told him that their friendship must end. Four days before the murder she told him quite definitely that she would not change her mind that there could be no question of a marriage.

Griffiths' familiarity with the hospital buildings and grounds was also established when it was discovered that he had spent two years there as a patient between the ages of ten and twelve. His hospital record showed that he was suffering at that time from incontinence of urine.

When Griffiths stood before Mr Justice Oliver and a jury at Lancaster Assizes on 15 October 1948, there was really only one issue to be decided — not whether he killed June Devaney but whether or not he was sane at the time.

Mr W. Gorman, KC, and Mr D. Brabin appeared for the Crown and Griffiths was defended by Mr Basil Nield, KC and Mr J. di V. Nahum.

Dr Gilbert Bailey, police surgeon for Blackburn, giving evidence for the prosecution, described the child's injuries and was cross-examined by Mr Nield.

* * *

'In the course of your thirty-four years in medical practice you have from time to time dealt with cases of violent death?' — 'Yes, many.'

'In your experience have you ever seen any injuries more consistent than those in this case with the outburst of a lunatic?' — 'I certainly consider the man who did this act must have been in a state of maniacal frenzy.'

'Does that mean in a condition of complete ferocity?' asked Mr Justice Oliver. Dr Bailey replied: 'Yes'.

The judge: 'A man is not necessarily mad because he acts in a ferocious manner?' — 'Not at all.'

'All you can say is that this was done by someone acting in a ferocious manner?' — 'At that time.'

Further questioned by Mr Nield, Dr Bailey said that the man who had murdered the child would be, in normal life, quite a normal man, but would have sudden outbursts of frenzy or mania. He had the impression that the man might be a schizophrenic. The motive in this case was an uncontrollable sexual impulse.

Mr Justice Oliver commented: 'There was a sexual motive here; whether sane or insane, the jury will decide'.

Mr Gorman, further examining Dr Bailey:

'You have been asked a number of theoretical considerations in this case; is it necessary before you can arrive at a proper view as to the condition of this man that you should have him for some time under observation?' — 'Yes. In this particular case, I would like to say now that I have not had this man under observation.

'I am not prepared to say what his true mentality is. All I am prepared to say is that the act of murder and rape on this child could have been the act of a man with a 'split' mind.'

Opening the case for the defence, Mr Nield said it was his submission that Griffiths, at the time of the murder, was mad and he added: 'I say to you frankly at this early stage that I cannot ask for this man's liberty, but I do ask for his life.'

There were, he said, six categories of evidence which would help the jury to decide whether Griffiths was sane or insane.

Firstly, there was his family history. In 1918, for a period of about nine months, his father had been in a mental hospital suffering from what was described at the time as 'delusional insanity' — a condition which in the more technical term of modern times was described as 'paranoid schizophrenia'.

Secondly, Peter Griffiths' own personal

history had to be considered. When he was six years old he fell from a milk-float upon his head, but a doctor was not called. Later he spent two years in hospital suffering from something about which there was little real information — incontinence of urine. Might there not have been some neurotic foundation for that long stay in hospital?

'Even at the age of seventeen this young man was childish in his habits,' continued Mr Nield. 'He would shut himself up in a room and play with corks, pretending they were trains. So noticeable was this that his mother rebuked him and said he was going mental. Thereafter there is a long history of solitary habits, always alone, depressed, and a typical picture of an incipient schizophrenic who might at any time fall under the blow of this disease in which, in a moment of maniacal frenzy, this sort of hideous happening can occur.'

Griffiths had left job after job, never remaining for more than a short time; as a boy he was unstable and stole things; his Army category was bad or indifferent and he deserted twice.

The third category of evidence, said Mr Nield, related to events immediately preceding the act — and one of these was the meeting with Miss Rene Edge, whom the young man wished to marry, when she told him for the second time that she was not prepared to go on with the friendship.

'You may have in the case of a schizophrenic a precipitating factor which may produce one of these frenzies,' he added, 'and an unhappy love affair is typical of such a disturbance.'

It was also quite plain that the accused had had a great deal too much to drink on 14 May, and medical testimony was that excessive alcohol might induce the mental disturbance.

The fourth consideration related to the act itself. It was recognized that an act of gross and hideous ferocity might well be an indication of mental disorder. 'Can you think of a case of more hideous ferocity than this?'

The events immediately after the act were to be considered in the fifth category.

'This man went away from that hospital, slept that night as if nothing had happened, and then went out with this young lady,' continued counsel. 'There was no effort to wash away any stains from his suit and there was that unnatural calm which goes with one who has had a mental breakdown of the nature I have suggested.'

The sixth category of evidence was that of the medical experts, said Mr Nield, who then called Dr Alistair Grant, of Whittingham

Mental Hospital and Dr Geoffrey Talbot, Medical Superintendent of Prestwich Hospital.

Dr Grant said that he had twice examined Griffiths and had formed the opinion that he was suffering from schizophrenia. One of his reasons for that belief was the question of heredity. The man's father had suffered from what was probably paranoid schizophrenia and in sixty per cent of schizophrenics heredity was given as a cause.

In reply to questions put by Mr Nield, Dr Grant said that solitary habits and childish behaviour were the sort of symptoms found in early schizophrenia. Constant changing of jobs was very typical. An unhappy or frustrated love affair could precipitate the condition and it was a well-known fact that schizophrenics reacted badly to alcohol.

Cross-examined by Mr Gorman about the statement Griffiths made after his arrest, Dr Grant said the man might not have recalled raping the child because he did not mention it.

Mr Justice Oliver: 'Why should he forget that if he remembered every other detail?'

Dr Grant: 'In a case of ordinary schizo-phrenia, I would be rather surprised to find that a man had remembered so much and yet forgotten such an important thing, but that is

171

the sort of partial amnesia you would get in a drunk.'

Mr Gorman: 'Is it not quite clear that the whole of that statement, with its details, with its lies, with its concealments, is the statement of an active mind appreciating what was being done at the time?' — 'Most of the points you have made I am in complete agreement with, but I do differ about the material time, the time when he murdered the child.'

'Will you tell me what there is in this statement that enables you to take a portion of time and say that within that portion of time this man was in this mental state?' — 'I am judging by my direct experience in these cases, and I again repeat that, in my opinion, it is quite possible for a man, having schizophrenia, to have a maniacal attack lasting a short time and to recover himself fairly quickly afterwards.'

Mr Justice Oliver: 'I want to ask you one thing. Do you regard the raping of even small children as evidence of insanity?' — 'No.'

'Is there anything mad in what he did — on the part of a man who had been brutal enough to ravish her — is there anything mad in beating her brains out to stop her screaming?' — 'I think so, for this reason, that she was a child, she would have no evidence

172

against him, and he could have got away.'

Dr Talbot gave evidence relating to the detention of Peter Griffiths senior in Prestwich Hospital and said that he was sent there by the Army as a dangerous lunatic soldier. The medical note entered on the record was a very good description of the condition now known as paranoid schizophrenia, which was known to be hereditary. Griffiths Senior had been discharged in 1919, after nine months, but that did not mean that he had been completely cured.

'My conclusion was that the type of mental illness from which he, the father, was suffering may have been regarded as hereditary and likely to appear in any or other of subsequent generations.' he concluded.

The fourth medical witness, Dr Francis Brisby, Principal Medical Officer at Liverpool Prison and former Assistant Medical Officer at a Lancaster county mental hospital appeared for the prosecution. He said that from observation and examination of the accused man he had found no evidence of any disease of the mind which would prevent him from either knowing what he was doing or that what he was doing was wrong. Cross-examined by Mr Nield, he said he did not think the evidence suggested a complete picture of schizophrenia. He would expect some alteration of character, some change in the man's personality occurring before the event, some history of conduct alien to his nature.

In his lengthy and detailed summing up to the jury, Mr Justice Oliver said it would seem to him a most amazing disease when the man could be perfectly sane right up to the moment he laid the child on the ground, then a schizophrenic maniac during the time he was raping her and beating her brains out, then perfectly sane afterwards and remain sane ever since.

'It does indeed seem to be a very odd sort of disease,' he said. 'We are only laymen, we have not got the knowledge of the experts. I do not know whether you find it difficult to envisage a man quite sane and knowing what he is doing when taking the child out of the hospital ward and walking with it into the grounds, and then suddenly becoming bereft of his senses and raping and killing, and then getting his senses back again. I do not know whether it seems to you to be more likely, if that is really true, that the man would have a blank and would say, 'All I remember is picking the child up and taking her out, and I cannot tell you what happened until I found myself at home.' That may, at any rate, seem more consistent with the facts here, but you are the judges, not I.'

The jury of nine men and three women were out only twenty-five minutes before giving their verdict of Guilty.

Passing sentence of death, Mr Justice Oliver said to Griffiths: 'The jury has found you guilty of a crime of the most brutal ferocity and I entirely agree with that verdict.' June Devaney's murderer was hanged in Walton Prison, Liverpool, on 19 November 1948. On the day before the execution he was interviewed by Superintendent Capstick and Detective Superintendent Lindsay, of Lancashire CID, who asked him if he had also killed Jack Quentin Smith.

Griffiths replied, 'No', but Capstick remained convinced that the ex-Guardsman was the 'moon maniac' of Lancashire and had been guilty of more than the one murder of which he was convicted.

DR PARKMAN TAKES A WALK

(Professor John Webster, USA 1849)

Cleveland Amory

This cautionary tale demonstrates that not only can scientists themselves stoop to murder, but that they can also be caught out by a simple scientific oversight. John White Webster was professor of chemistry and mineralogy at Massachusetts Medical College. He was a well-respected academic but he lived beyond his means, and borrowed money to fund his extravagant lifestyle. Webster became indebted to Dr George Parkman, who had given up a medical career to make a fortune in real estate dealings, and who was pressing Webster for his money. In a rage, Professor Webster murdered the miserly Parkman and burned the body in his assay oven. Webster was caught because the flames failed to consume Parkman's false teeth, which were found in the ashes. Cleveland Amory (1917–98) was a social historian who began his career as a newspaper reporter, becoming associate editor of the Saturday Evening Post. A self-proclaimed curmudgeon, he hosted a hugely-popular radio show Curmudgeon at Large. *This account of the Webster-Parkman case comes from his 1947 book* The Proper Bostonians *which scrutinized the wealthier and better-connected of Boston's residents.*

To the student of American Society the year 1849 will always remain a red-letter one. In that year two events occurred at opposite ends of the country, both of which, in their own way, made social history. At one end, in Sutter's Creek, California, gold was discovered. At the other, in Boston, Massachusetts, Dr George Parkman walked off the face of the earth.

The discovery of gold ushered in a new social era. It marked the first great rise of the Western *nouveau riche*, the beginning of that wonderful time when a gentleman arriving in San Francisco and offering a boy fifty cents to carry his suitcase could receive the reply, 'Here's a dollar, man — carry it yourself,' and when a poor Irish prospector suddenly striking it rich in a vein near Central City, Colorado, could fling down his pick and exclaim, 'Thank God, now my wife can be a lady!'

Dr Parkman's little walk did no such thing as this. It must be remembered, however, that it occurred some 3,000 miles away. Boston is not Sutter's Creek or Central City or even San Francisco. There has never been a 'new' social era in the Western sense in Boston's rock-ribbed Society, and it remains very doubtful if there ever will be one. The best that could be expected of any one event in Boston would be to shake up the old. Dr Parkman's walk did this; it shook Boston Society to the very bottom of its First Family foundations. Viewed almost a hundred years later it thus seems, in its restricted way, almost as wonderful as the Gold Rush and not undeserving of the accidental fact that it happened, in the great march of social history, in exactly the same year.

The date was Friday, November 23rd. It was warm for a Boston November, and Dr Parkman needed no overcoat as he left his Beacon Hill home at 8 Walnut Street. He wore in the fashion of the day a black morning coat, purple silk vest, dark trousers, a dark-figured black tie, and a black silk top hat. He had breakfasted as usual, and he left his home to head down town toward the Merchants Bank on State Street. Dr Parkman was quite a figure as he moved along. His high hat and angular physique made him seem far taller than his actual five feet nine and a half inches. He was sixty years old and his head was almost bald, but his hat hid this fact also. To all outward appearances he was remarkably well-preserved, his most striking feature being a conspicuously protruding chin. Boston Parkmans have been noted for their chins the way Boston Adamses are noted for their foreheads or Boston Salton-stalls are noted for their noses, and the chin of old Dr Parkman was especially formidable. His lower jaw jutted out so far it had made the fitting of a set of false teeth for him a very difficult job. The dentist who had had that job had never forgotten it. He was proud of the china-white teeth he had installed. He had even kept the mould to prove to people that he, little Dr Nathan Keep, had made the teeth of the great Dr George Parkman.

Although he had studied to be a physician and received his degree Dr Parkman had rarely practised medicine in his life. He was a merchant at heart, one of Boston's wealthiest men, and he spent his time in the Boston manner keeping sharp account of his money — and a sharp eye on his debtors. He had many of the traits of character peculiar to the Proper Bostonian breed. He was shrewd and hard, but he was Boston-honest, Boston-direct and Boston-dependable. Like so many other First Family men before his time and after Dr Parkman was not popular but he was highly respected. It was hard to like a man like Dr Parkman because his manners were curt and he had a way of glaring at people that made them uncomfortable. Without liking him, however, it was possible to look up to him. People knew him as a great philanthropist and it was said he had given away a hundred thousand dollars in his time. The phrase 'wholesale charity and retail penury' as descriptive of the Proper Bostonian breed had not yet come into the Boston lingo, though the day was coming when Dr Parkman might be regarded as the very personification of it. Certainly he had given away large sums of money with wholesale generosity — even anonymously — yet with small sums, with money on a retail basis, he was penny-punctilious. 'The same rule,' a biographer records, 'governed Dr Parkman in settling an account involving the balance of a cent as in transactions of thousands of dollars.'

Children in the Boston streets pointed out Dr Parkman to other children. 'There goes Dr Parkman,' they would say. People always seemed to point him out after he had passed them. There was no use speaking to Dr Parkman before he went by. If you weren't his friend, Dr George Shattuck, or his brother-in-law, Robert Gould Shaw, Esq, or a Cabot or a Lowell, or perhaps a man who owed him money — and then, as someone said, God help you — the doctor would ignore you. Dr Parkman had no need to court favor from anybody. The Parkmans cut a sizeable chunk of Boston's social ice in 1849, and they still do today. Like other merchant-blooded First Families they were of course economically self-sufficient. They hadn't yet made much of an intellectual mark on their city, but a nephew of the doctor, Francis Parkman, had just published his first book and was on his way to becoming what Van Wyck Brooks has called 'the climax and crown' of the Boston historical school. The Parkmans were in the Boston fashion well-connected by marriages. Dr Parkman's sister's marriage with Robert Gould Shaw, Boston's wealthiest merchant, was a typical First Family alliance. As for Dr Parkman's own wealth, some idea of its extent may be gathered from the fact that his son, who never worked a day in his life, was able to leave a will which bequeathed, among other things, the sum of five million dollars for the care and improvement of the Boston Common.

On the morning of that Friday, November

23rd, Dr Parkman was hurrying. He walked with the characteristic gait of the Proper Bostonian merchant — a gait still practised by such notable present-day First Family footmen as Charles Francis Adams and Godfrey Lowell Cabot — measuring off distances with long, ground-consuming strides. Dr Parkman always hurried. Once when riding a horse up Beacon Hill and unable to speed the animal to his satisfaction he had left the horse in the middle of the street and hurried ahead on foot. On that occasion he had been after money, a matter of debt collection.

This morning, too, Dr Parkman was after money. He left the Merchants Bank and after making several other calls dropped into a grocery store at the corner of Blossom and Vine Streets. This stop, the only non-financial mission of his morning, was to buy a head of lettuce for his invalid sister. He left it in the store and said he would return for it on his way home. The time was half past one and Dr Parkman presumably intended to be home at 2.30, then the fashionable hour for one's midday meal. Ten minutes later, at 1.40, Elias Fuller, a merchant standing outside his counting room at Fuller's Iron Foundry at the corner of Vine and North Grove Streets, observed Dr Parkman passing him headed north on North Grove Street. Fuller was later to remember that the doctor seemed particularly annoyed about something and recalled that his cane beat a brisk tattoo on the pavement as he hurried along. What the merchant observed at 1.40 that day is of more than passing importance, for Elias Fuller was the last man who ever saw the doctor alive on the streets of Boston. Somewhere, last seen going north on North Grove Street, Dr George Parkman walked off the face of the earth.

At 8 Walnut Street Mrs Parkman, her daughter Harriet and Dr Parkman's invalid sister sat down to their two-thirty dinner long after three o'clock. Their dinner was ruined and there was no lettuce, but Mrs Parkman and the others did not mind. They were all worried about the master of the house. Dr Parkman was not the sort of man who was ever late for anything. Right after dinner they got in touch with Dr Parkman's agent, Charles Kingsley. Kingsley was the man who looked after the doctor's business affairs, usually some time after the doctor had thoroughly looked after them himself. Almost at once Kingsley began to search for his employer. First Family men of the promi- nence of Dr Parkman did not disappear in Boston — and they do not today — even for an afternoon. By night-fall Kingsley was ready to inform Robert Gould Shaw. Shaw, acting with the customary dispatch of the Proper Bostonian merchant, went at once to Boston's City Marshal, Mr Tukey. Marshal Tukey did of course what Shaw told him to do, which was to instigate an all-night search.

The next morning the merchant Shaw placed advertisements in all the papers and had 28,000 handbills distributed. The advertisements and the handbills announced a reward of $3,000 for his brother-in-law alive and $1,000 for his brother-in-law dead. The prices, considering the times, were sky-high but Shaw knew what he was doing in Yankee Boston. Before long virtually every able-bodied man, woman and child in the city was looking for Dr Parkman. They beat the bushes and they combed the streets. Slum areas were ransacked. All suspicious characters, all persons with known criminal records, were rounded up and held for questioning. Strangers in Boston were given a summary one-two treatment. An Irishman, it is recorded, attempting to change a twenty-dollar bill, was brought in to the police headquarters apparently solely on the assumption that no son of Erin, in the Boston of 1849, had any business with a bill of this size in his possession.

Every one of Dr Parkman's actions on the

previous day, up to 1.40, were checked. At that time, on North Grove Street, the trail always ended. Police had to sift all manner of wild reports. One had the doctor 'beguiled to East Cambridge and done in.' Another had him riding in a hansom cab, his head covered with blood, being driven at 'breakneck speed' over a Charles River bridge. Of the papers only the Boston *Transcript* seems to have kept its head. Its reporter managed to learn from a servant in the Parkman home that the doctor had received a caller at 9.30 Friday reminding him of a 1.30 appointment later in the day. The servant could not remember what the man looked like, but the *Transcript* printed the story in its Saturday night edition along with the reward advertisements. Most people took the caller to be some sort of front man who had appeared to lead Dr Parkman to a dastardly death. By Monday foul play was so thoroughly suspected that the shrewd merchant Shaw saw no reason to mention a sum as high as $1,000 for the body. Three thousand dollars was still the price for Dr Parkman alive but only 'a suitable reward' was mentioned in Shaw's Monday handbills for Dr Parkman dead. Monday's handbills also noted the possibility of amnesia but the theory of a First Family man's mind wandering to this extent was regarded as highly doubtful. Dr Parkman, it was stated, was 'perfectly well' when he left his house.

All that the Parkman case now needed to make it a complete panorama of Boston's First Family Society was the active entry of Harvard College into the picture. This occurred on Sunday morning in the person of a caller to the home of Rev. Francis Parkman, the missing doctor's brother, where the entire Family Parkman in all its ramifications had gathered. The caller was a man named John White Webster, Harvard graduate and professor of chemistry at the Harvard Medical School. He was a short squat man, fifty-six years old, who had a mass of unruly black hair and always wore thick spectacles. He had had a most distinguished career. He had studied at Guy's Hospital, London, back in 1815, where among his fellow students had been the poet John Keats. He was a member of the London Geological Society, the American Academy of Arts and Sciences, and during his twenty-five years as a Harvard professor had published numerous nationally noted scientific works. His wife, a Hickling and aunt of the soon-to-be-recognized historian William Hickling Prescott, was 'well-connected' with several of Boston's First Families.

The Rev. Parkman was glad to see

Professor Webster and ushered him toward the parlour expecting that his desire would be to offer sympathy to the assorted Parkmans there assembled. But Webster, it seemed, did not want to go into the parlour. Instead he spoke abruptly to the minister. 'I have come to tell you,' he said, 'that I saw your brother at half past one o'clock on Friday.' The minister was glad to have this report. Since Webster also told him he had been the caller at the Parkman home earlier that day it cleared up the mystery of the strange appointment as recorded in the *Transcript*. Webster explained he should have come sooner but had been so busy he had not seen the notices of Dr Parkman's disappearance until the previous night. The minister was also satisfied with this. Webster further declared that, at the appointment shortly after 1.30 which took place in his laboratory at the Medical School, he had paid Dr Parkman the sum of $483.64 which he had owed him. This, of course, explained why the doctor had last been seen by the merchant Fuller in such a cane-tattooing hurry. It had indeed been a matter of a debt collection.

When Professor Webster had left, Robert Gould Shaw was advised of his visit. Shaw was intimate enough in his brother-in-law's affairs to know that Webster had been owing

Dr Parkman money for some time. He did not, however, know the full extent of Webster's misery. Few men have ever suffered from the retail penury side of the Proper Bostonian character as acutely as John White Webster.

The professor received a salary from Harvard of $1,200 a year. This, augmented by income from extra lectures he was able to give, might have sufficed for the average Harvard professor in those days. But Webster was not the average. His wife, for all her connections with Boston's First Families, was still a socially aspirant woman, particularly for her two daughters of debutante age. Mrs Webster and the Misses Webster entertained lavishly at their charming home in Cambridge. Professor Webster went into debt. He borrowed money here and he borrowed money there. But mostly he borrowed from Dr George Parkman.

Who better to borrow from? Dr Parkman, man of wholesale charity, Proper Bostonian merchant philanthropist. He had given Harvard College the very ground on which at that time stood its Medical School. He had endowed the Parkman Chair of Anatomy, then being occupied by the great Dr Oliver Wendell Holmes. He had himself been responsible for Webster's appointment as chemistry professor. There were no two ways about it. When Webster needed money the doctor was his obvious choice. As early as 1842 he had borrowed $400. He had then borrowed more. In 1847 he had borrowed from a group headed by Dr Parkman the sum of $2,000. For the latter he had been forced to give a mortgage on all his personal property. He knew he had little chance to pay the debt but he was banking on the generosity of the 'good Dr Parkman.' A year later, in 1848, he even went to Dr Parkman's brother-in-law, the merchant Shaw, and prevailed upon him to buy a mineral collection for $1,200. This was most unfortunate. The mineral collection, like the rest of Webster's property, in hock to Dr Parkman and his group, was not Webster's to sell. By so doing he had made the doctor guilty of that cardinal sin of Yankeeism — the sin of being shown up as an easy mark. No longer was there for Webster any 'good Dr Parkman.' 'From that moment onward,' says author Stewart Holbrook, 'poor Professor Webster knew what it was like to have a Yankee bloodhound on his trail. His creditor was a punctilious man who paid his own obligations when due and he expected the same of everybody else, even a Harvard professor.'

Dr Parkman dogged Professor Webster in

the streets, outside his home, even to the classrooms. He would come in and take a front-row seat at Webster's lectures. He would not say anything; he would just sit and glare in that remarkable way of his. He wrote the professor notes, not just plain insulting notes but the awful, superior, skin-biting notes of the Yankee gentleman. He spoke sternly of legal processes. Meeting Webster he would never shout at him but instead address him in clipped Proper Bostonian accents. It was always the same question. When would the professor be 'ready' for him?

Dr Parkman even bearded Professor Webster in his den, in the inner recesses of the latter's laboratory at the Medical School. He had been there, in the professor's private back room — according to the janitor of the building — on Monday evening, November 19th, just four days before he had disappeared.

The janitor was a strange man, the grim New England village type, a small person with dark brooding eyes. His name was Ephraim Littlefield. He watched with growing interest the goings-on around him. Following Webster's call on Rev. Francis Parkman, which established the farthest link yet on the trail of Dr Parkman's walk, it had of course been necessary to search the

Medical School. Littlefield wanted this done thoroughly, as thoroughly for example as they were dragging the Charles River outside. He personally led the investigators to Webster's laboratory. Everything was searched, all but the private back room and adjoining privy. One of the party of investigators, which also included Dr Parkman's agent Kingsley, was a police officer named Derastus Clapp. Littlefield prevailed upon this officer to go in to the back room, but just as Clapp opened the door Professor Webster solicitously called out for him to be careful. There were dangerous articles in there, he said. 'Very well, then,' said Officer Clapp, 'I will not go in there and get blowed up.' He backed out again.

The whole search was carried on to the satisfaction of even Robert Gould Shaw who, after all, knew at firsthand the story of Webster's duplicity via the mineral collection. And who was the little janitor Ephraim Littlefield to dispute the word of the great merchant Robert Shaw? As each day went by the theory of murder was becoming more and more generally accepted, but in a Boston Society eternally geared to the mesh of a Harvard A.B. degree the idea of pinning a homicide on a Harvard man — and a professor at that — was heresy itself. One might as well pry for the body of Dr Parkman among the prayer cushions of the First Family pews in Trinity Church.

But Littlefield was not, in the socially sacrosanct meaning of the words, a 'Harvard man.' He was a Harvard janitor. Furthermore he was stubborn. He wanted the Medical School searched again. When it was, he was once more prodding the investigators to greater efforts. He told them they should visit the cellar of the building, down in the section where the Charles River water flowed in and carried off waste matter from the dissecting rooms and privies above. The agent Kingsley took one gentlemanly sniff from the head of the stairs and refused to accompany the janitor and the other investigators any farther. The others, however, went on. As they passed the wall under Webster's back room the janitor volunteered the information that it was now the only place in the building that hadn't been searched. Why not, the men wanted to know. The janitor explained that to get there it would be necessary to dig through the wall. The men had little stomach left for this sort of operation and soon rejoined Kingsley upstairs.

Littlefield, however, had plenty of stomach. He determined to dig into the wall himself. Whether he was by this time, Monday, already suspicious of Professor Webster has never been made clear. He had, it is true, heard the Webster-Parkman meeting of Monday night the week before. He had distinctly overheard the doctor say to the professor in that ever-insinuating way, 'Something, Sir, must be accomplished.' Just yesterday, Sunday, he had seen Professor Webster enter the Medical School around noontime, apparently shortly after he had made his call on Rev. Francis Parkman. Webster had spoken to him and had acted 'very queerly.' Come to think of it, Littlefield brooded, Sunday was a queer day for the professor to be hanging around the School anyway. 'Ephraim,' writes Richard Dempewolff, one of the Parkman case's most avid devotees, 'was one of those shrewd New England conclusion-jumpers who, unfortunately for the people they victimize, are usually right. By putting two and two together, Mr Littlefield achieved a nice round dozen.'

The janitor's wife was a practical woman. She thought little of her husband's determination to search the filthy old place under the private rooms of the Harvard professor she had always regarded as a fine gentleman. Her husband would lose this job, that would be what would happen. Just you wait and see, Mr Littlefield.

Mr Littlefield deferred to Mrs Littlefield and did wait — until Tuesday, five days after Dr Parkman's disappearance. On Tuesday something extraordinary happened. At four o'clock in the afternoon he heard Professor Webster's bell jangle, a signal that the janitor was wanted. He went to Webster's laboratory. The professor asked him if he had bought his Thanksgiving turkey yet. Littlefield did not know what to say. He replied he had thought some about going out Thanksgiving.

'Here,' said Webster, 'go and get yourself one.' With that he handed the janitor an order for a turkey at a nearby grocery store.

John White Webster had here made a fatal error. The call he had paid on Rev. Francis Parkman had been bad enough. It had aroused the searching of the Medical School and had brought Littlefield actively into the case. But as Webster later admitted he had been afraid that sooner or later someone would have found out about his 1.30 Friday rendezvous with Dr Parkman and felt that his best chance lay in making a clean breast of it. For this action in regard to the janitor's Thanksgiving turkey, however, there could be no such defence. If he hoped to win the janitor over to 'his side,' then he was a poor judge of human nature indeed. Harvard Janitor Ephraim Littlefield had worked for

Harvard Professor John Webster for seven years — curiously the same length of time Professor John Webster had been borrowing from Dr Parkman — without ever receiving a present of any kind. And now, a Thanksgiving turkey. Even the deferentially dormant suspicions of Mrs Littlefield were thoroughly aroused.

Janitor Littlefield had no chance to begin his labours Wednesday. Professor Webster was in his laboratory most of the day. On Thanksgiving, however, while Mrs Littlefield kept her eyes peeled for the professor or any other intruder, the janitor began the task of crow-barring his way through the solid brick wall below the back room. It was slow work and even though the Littlefields took time off to enjoy their dinner — the janitor had characteristically not passed up the opportunity to procure a nine-pound bird — it was soon obvious he could not get through the wall in one day. That evening the Littlefields took time off again. They went to a dance given by the Sons of Temperance Division of the Boston Odd Fellows. They stayed until four o'clock in the morning. 'There were twenty dances,' Littlefield afterwards recalled, 'and I danced eighteen out of the twenty.'

Late Friday afternoon, after Professor Webster had left for the day, Littlefield was at his digging again. This time he had taken the precaution of advising two of the School's First Family doctors, Doctors Bigelow and Jackson, of what he was doing. They were surprised but told him since he had started he might as well continue. But they were against his idea of informing the dean of the School, Dr Holmes, of the matter. It would, they felt, disturb the dean unnecessarily.

Even a half-hearted First Family blessing has always counted for something in Boston, and Janitor Littlefield now went to work with renewed vigour. Again his wife stood watch. At five-thirty he broke through the fifth of the five courses of brick in the wall. 'I held my light forward,' he afterwards declared, 'and the first thing which I saw was the pelvis of a man, and two parts of a leg . . . It was no place for these things.'

It was not indeed. Within fifteen minutes Doctors Bigelow and Jackson were on the scene. Later Dr Holmes himself would view the remains. Meanwhile of course there was the matter of a little trip out to the Webster home in Cambridge.

To that same police officer who had been so loath to get himself 'blowed up' in Webster's back room fell the honour of making the business trip to Cambridge and arresting the Harvard professor. Once bitten,

196

Derastus Clapp was twice shy. There would be no more monkeyshines, Harvard or no Harvard. He had his cab halt some distance from the Webster home and approached on foot. Opening the outer gate he started up the walk just as Webster himself appeared on the steps of his house, apparently showing a visitor out. The professor attempted to duck back inside. Officer Clapp hailed him. 'We are about to search the Medical School again,' he called, moving forward rapidly as he spoke, 'and we wish you to be present.' Webster feigned the traditional Harvard indifference. It was a waste of time; the School had already been searched twice. Clapp laid a stern hand on his shoulder. Webster, escorted outward and suddenly noting two other men in the waiting cab, wanted to go back for his keys. Officer Clapp was not unaware of the drama of the moment. 'Professor Webster,' he said, 'we have keys enough to unlock the whole of Harvard College.'

Boston was in an uproar. Dr Parkman had not walked off the face of the earth. He had been pushed off — and by the authoritative hands of a Harvard professor! Even the *Transcript*, calm when there was still a hope the Parkman case was merely a matter of disappearance, could restrain itself no longer. It threw its genteel caution to the winds.

There were two exclamation marks after its headline, and its editor called on Shakespeare himself to sum up the situation:

Since last evening, our whole population has been in a state of the greatest possible excitement in consequence of the astounding rumor that the body of Dr Parkman has been discovered, and that Dr John W. Webster, Professor of Chemistry in the Medical School of Harvard College, and a gentleman connected by marriage with some of our most distinguished families, has been arrested and imprisoned, on suspicion of being the murderer. Incredulity, then amazement, and then blank, unspeakable horror have been the emotions, which have agitated the public mind as the rumor has gone on, gathering countenance and confirmation. Never in the annals of crime in Massachusetts has such a sensation been produced.

In the streets, in the market-place, at every turn, men greet each other with pale, eager looks and the inquiry, 'Can it be true?' And then as the terrible reply, 'the circumstances begin to gather weight against him,' is wrung forth, the agitated listener can only vent his sickening sense of horror, in some expression as that of Hamlet, —

'O, horrible! O, horrible! most horrible!'

There is irony in the fact that proud, staid Boston chose the time it did to provide American Society with the nineteenth century's outstanding social circus. Boston was at the height of its cultural attainments in 1849. In that year a scholarly but hardly earth-shaking book by a rather minor Boston author *The History of Spanish Literature* by George Ticknor, was the world literary event of the year and the only book recommended by Lord Macaulay to Queen Victoria. Yet just three months later, on March 19, 1850, Boston put on a show which for pure social artistry Barnum himself would have had difficulty matching. The Boston courtroom had everything. It had one of Boston's greatest jurists, Judge Lemuel Shaw, on its bench; it had the only Harvard professor ever to be tried for murder, John White Webster, as its defendant; it had promised witnesses of national renown, from Dr Oliver Wendell Holmes on down; and in the offing, so to speak, it had the shades of Dr George

Parkman, perhaps the most socially distinguished victim in the annals of American crime.

Nobody wanted to miss such a sight. Trains and stages from all parts of the East brought people to Boston. They wanted tickets. Everybody in Boston wanted tickets, too. Consequences of revolutionary proportions were feared if they could not be accommodated. Yet what to do? There was only a small gallery to spare, it having been decreed in typical Boston fashion that the main part of the courtroom would be reserved on an invitation basis. Finally, Field Marshal Tukey hit on the only possible solution, which was to effect a complete change of audience in the gallery every ten minutes during the proceedings. It took elaborate street barricades and doorway defences to do the job, but in the eleven days of the trial, to that little gallery holding hardly more than a hundred souls, came a recorded total of 60,000 persons. Considering that the constabulary of Boston assigned to the job numbered just fifteen men, this feat ranks as a monumental milestone in police annals.

From the suspense angle the trial, which has been called a landmark in the history of criminal law, must have been something of a disappointment. By the time it began, despite

Webster's protestations of innocence, there was little doubt in the minds of most of the spectators as to the guilt of the professor, A few days after his arrest a skeleton measuring 70½ inches had finally been assembled from the grisly remains found lying about under the professor's back room, and while the sum total of this was an inch taller than Dr Parkman had been in happier days, there had been no question in the minds of the coroner's jury, of Dr Holmes, and of a lot of other people, but that Dr Parkman it was. The case against the professor was one of circumstantial evidence of course. No one had seen Webster and Parkman together at the time of the murder; indeed, during the trial the time of the murder was never satisfactorily established. But the strongest Webster adherents had to admit that it was evidence of a very powerful nature, as Chief Justice Shaw could not fail to point out in his famous charge to the jury, an address which lawyers today still consider one of the greatest expositions of the nature and use of circumstantial evidence ever delivered.

There were a number of pro-Websterites. Harvard professor though he may have been, he was still the underdog, up against the almighty forces of Boston's First Families. Many of the Websterites had undoubtedly had experiences of their own on the score of Proper Bostonian retail penury and were ready to recognize that Dr Parkman had been so importunate a creditor that he had quite possibly driven the little professor first to distraction and then to the deed. They went to Rufus Choate, Boston's great First Family lawyer, and asked him to undertake the defence. After reading up on the case Choate was apparently willing to do so on the condition that Webster would admit the killing and plead manslaughter. Another First Family lawyer, old Judge Fay, with whom the Webster family regularly played whist, thought a verdict of manslaughter could be reached.

But Webster would not plead guilty. From the beginning he had made his defence an all but impossible task. He talked when he shouldn't have talked and he kept quiet when, at least by the light of hindsight, he should have come clean. On his first trip to the jail he immediately asked the officers about the finding of the body. 'Have they found the *whole* body?' he wanted to know. This while certainly a reasonable question in view of the wide area over which the remains were found was hardly the thing for a man in his position to be asking. Then, while vehemently protesting his innocence, he took a strychnine pill out of his waistcoat pocket and attempted to kill himself, an attempt which was foiled only by the fact that, though the dose was a large one, he was in such a nervous condition it failed to take fatal effect. At the trial Webster maintained through his lawyers that the body he was proved to be so vigorously dismembering during his spare moments in the week following November 23rd had been a Medical School cadaver brought to him for that purpose. This was sheer folly, and the prosecution had but to call upon the little dentist, Nathan Keep, to prove it so. Tooth by tooth, during what was called one of the 'tumultuous moments' of the trial, Dr Keep fitted the fragments of the false teeth found in Webster's furnace into the mould he still had in his possession. Charred as they were there could be no doubt they had once been the china-white teeth of Dr Parkman.

The spectators were treated to other memorable scenes. The great Dr Holmes testified twice, once for the State on the matter, of the identity of the reconstructed skeleton and once for the defence as a character witness for the accused. Professor Webster's character witnesses were a howitzer battery of First Family notables, among them Doctors Bigelow and Jackson, a Codman and a Lovering, the New England historian John Gorham Palfrey and Nathaniel Bowditch, son of the famed mathematician — even Harvard's president Jared Sparks took the stand for his errant employee. All seemed to agree that Webster, if occasionally irritable, was basically a kindhearted man, and President Sparks was thoughtful enough to add one gratuitous comment. 'Our professors,' he said, 'do not often commit murder.'

Credit was due Webster for his ability as a cadaver carver. He had done the job on Dr Parkman, it was established, with no more formidable instrument than a jackknife. A Dr Woodbridge Strong was especially emphatic on this point. He had dissected a good many bodies in his time, he recalled, including a rush job on a decaying pirate, but never one with just a jackknife. Ephraim Littlefield was of course star witness for the prosecution. The indefatigable little janitor talked for one whole day on the witness stand, a total of eight hours, five hours in the morning before recess for lunch and three hours in the afternoon. Only once did he falter and that on the occasion when, under cross-examination with the defence making a valiant attempt to throw suspicion on him, he was asked if he played 'gambling cards' with friends in Webster's back room. Four times the defence had to ask the question and four times Littlefield refused to answer. Finally, his New England conscience stung to the quick, he replied in exasperation, 'If you ask me if I played cards there *last winter*, I can truthfully say I did not.'

In those days prisoners were not allowed to testify, but on the last day of the trial Professor Webster was asked if he wanted to say anything. Against the advice of his counsel he rose and spoke for fifteen minutes. He spent most of those precious moments denying the accusation that he had written the various anonymous notes which had been turning up from time to time in the City Marshal's office ever since the disappearance of Dr Parkman. One of these had been signed CIVIS and Webster's last sentence was a pathetic plea for CIVIS to come forward if he was in the courtroom. CIVIS did not, and at eight o'clock on the evening of March 30th the trial was over.

Even the jury seems to have been overcome with pity for the professor. Before filing out of the courtroom the foreman, pointing a trembling finger at Webster, asked: 'is that all? Is that the end? Can nothing further be said in defence of the man?' Three hours later the foreman and his cohorts were back, having spent, it is recorded, the first two hours and fifty-five minutes in prayer 'to put off the sorrowful duty.' When the verdict was delivered, 'an awful and unbroken silence ensued, in which the Court, the jury, the clerk, and the spectators seemed to be absorbed in their own reflections.'

★ ★ ★

Webster's hanging, by the neck and until he was dead, proceeded without untoward incident in the courtyard of Boston's Leverett Street jail just five months to the day after he had been declared guilty. Before that time, however, the professor made a complete confession. He stated that Dr Parkman had come into his laboratory on that fatal Friday and that, when he had been unable to produce the money he owed, the doctor had shown him a sheaf of papers proving that he had been responsible for getting him his professorship. The doctor then added, 'I got you into your office, Sir, and now I will get you out of it.' This, said Webster, so infuriated him that he seized a stick of wood off his laboratory bench and struck Dr Parkman one blow on the head. Death was instantaneous and Webster declared, 'I saw nothing but the alternative of a successful removal and concealment of the body, on the one hand,

and of infamy and destruction on the other.' He then related his week-long attempt to dismember and burn the body. Even the clergyman who regularly visited Webster in his cell during his last days was not able to extract from the professor the admission that the crime had been premeditated. He had done it in that one frenzy of rage. 'I am irritable and passionate,' the clergyman quoted Webster as saying, 'and Dr Parkman was the most provoking of men.'

The late Edmund Pearson, recognized authority on non-fictional homicide here and abroad, has called the Webster — Parkman case America's classic murder and the one which has lived longest in books of reminiscence. Certainly in Boston's First Family Society the aftermath of the case has been hardly less distinguished than its actual occurrence. To this day no Proper Bostonian grandfather autobiography is complete without some reference to the case. The Beacon Hill house at 8 Walnut Street from which Dr Parkman started out on his walk that Friday morning almost a hundred years ago is still standing, and its present occupant, a prominent Boston lawyer, is still on occasion plagued by the never-say-die curious.

Among Boston Parkmans the effect was a profound one. For years certain members of the Family shrank from Society altogether, embarrassed as they were by the grievous result of Dr Parkman's financial punctiliousness and all too aware of the sympathy extended Professor Webster in his budgetary plight. In the doctor's immediate family it is noteworthy that his widow headed the subscription list of a fund taken up to care for Webster's wife and children. Dr Parkman's son, George Francis Parkman, was five years out of Harvard in 1849. He had been, in contrast to his father, a rather gay blade as a youth and at college had taken part in Hasty Pudding Club theatricals; at the time of the murder he was enjoying himself in Paris. He returned to Boston a marred man. He moved his mother and sister from 8 Walnut Street and took a house at 33 Beacon Street. From the latter house he buried his mother and aunt, and there he and his sister lived on as Boston Society's most distinguished recluses. His solitary existence never included even the solace of a job. Describing him as he appeared a full fifty years after the crime a biographer records:

Past the chain of the bolted door on Beacon Street no strangers, save those who came on easily recognised business, were ever allowed to enter. Here George

Francis Parkman and his sister Harriet, neither of whom ever married, practised the utmost frugality, the master of the house going himself to the market every day to purchase their meager provisions, and invariably paying cash for the simple supplies he brought home.

The windows of his house looked out upon the Common but he did not frequent it . . . He always walked slowly and alone, in a stately way, and attracted attention by his distinguished though retiring appearance . . . In cool weather he wore a heavy coat of dark cloth and his shoulders and neck were closely wrapped with a wide scarf, the ends of which were tucked into his coat or under folds. He sheltered himself against the east winds of Boston just as he seemed, by his manner, to shelter his inmost self from contact with the ordinary affairs of men.

Tremors of the Parkman earthquake continued to be felt by Boston Society often at times when they were least desired. Twenty years later, when Boston was privileged to play proud host to Charles Dickens, there was a particularly intense tremor. Dickens was asked which one of the city's historic landmarks he would like to visit first. 'The room where Dr Parkman was murdered,' he replied, and there being no doubt he meant what he said, nothing remained for a wry-faced group of Boston's best but to shepherd the distinguished novelist out to the chemistry laboratory of the Harvard Medical School.

A Webster-Parkman story, vintage of 1880, is still told today by Boston's distinguished author and teacher, Bliss Perry. He recalls that for a meeting of New England college officers at Williamstown, Massachusetts, his mother had been asked to put up as a guest in her house Boston's First Family poet laureate, diplomat and first editor of the *Atlantic*, James Russell Lowell. Unfortunately Lowell was at that time teaching at Harvard and for all his other accomplishments Mrs Perry would have none of him. He had to be quartered elsewhere.

'I could not sleep,' Mrs Perry said, 'if one of those Harvard professors were in the house.'

THE MURDERER WHO GOT AWAY WITH IT

(John Donald Merrett, UK 1926)

Macdonald Hastings

This case presents one of the few occasions in which a human ear — that of a murder victim — was produced in court as evidence. John Donald Merrett was only eighteen when he was tried for the murder of his mother. Mrs Merrett had been found in her sitting room with a bullet hole above her right ear. Her son, who inherited a fortune on her death, claimed she had shot herself. At the young man's trial, the Crown's ballistics experts claimed that the wound could not have been self-inflicted. For one thing, Mrs Merrett could not have mustered the strength needed to pull the trigger, and for another, there were no powder burns around the bullet hole. The opinion of the experts was that such burns would have been there if the gun had been fired at close range by Mrs Merrett herself. The celebrated pathologist Sir Bernard Spilsbury, appearing for once for the defence, disagreed. He testified that it was quite possible for the wound to have been self-inflicted, explaining the absence of powder burns by pointing out that they would have been washed away by bleeding and in the course of cleaning the wound. Although the case against young Merrett was strong — he had also forged his mother's signature on several hundred pounds'-worth of cheques — the jury felt unable to disregard the sworn evidence of the great Spilsbury. Because the case was tried in Scotland, they were able to return a verdict of Not Proven on the murder charge. (Merrett was convicted of forgery and was jailed for a year). Merrett resurfaced as Ronald Chesney more than a quarter of a century later, when he killed his wife and mother-in-law and finally himself. The Merrett case was told by the writer and broadcaster Macdonald Hastings (1909–82) in his biography of Robert Churchill, the ballistics expert whose evidence featured in many British murder trials in the 1920s and 1930s.

The newspaper headline, 'NOW IT CAN BE TOLD,' on February 17, 1954, announced that a controversy of the criminal courts which had been the cause of debate, often bitter debate, for twenty-eight years was at last resolved. Churchill and Spilsbury were two of the central figures in the argument. The case was essentially a conflict between experts, one which subsequently lent weight to murmurings of doubt as to what value could be reposed on the evidence of specialist witnesses. To make a cool assessment of it, the story of the nefarious career of John Donald Merrett is one which is best considered, not from its beginning, but from its end.

On February 16, 1954, Ronald John Chesney, one of several aliases which John Donald Merrett adopted during his life, was found shot dead through the mouth in a wood on the outskirts of Cologne. A Colt automatic, an ugly weapon which blew off the top of his head, lay at his side. He had committed suicide; and none too soon. He was wanted for the murder of his wife and mother-in-law, who ran an Old Folks' Home in the normally safe respectability of the London suburb of Ealing.

He killed his wife with the intention of obtaining a sum of money he had settled on her many years before which he himself had inherited from his mother after she too had had a violent end. He killed his mother-in-law because she had the misfortune to discover him when he was faking the appearance that his wife's death was accidental.

It was a disappointing outcome for him, because he had put himself to some trouble to prove that he could not have had any part in the affair. He had previously made a visit to England from Germany, a country where he had business interests and a girlfriend, during which he stole a passport from a man he met in a pub, and made a sufficient exhibition of himself at the port of departure to secure that he had an alibi. He subsequently returned on the stolen passport. His wife's murder — he sank her body in a bath — might possibly have passed as an accident if his mother-in-law hadn't interrupted him.

Thereafter it was only a matter of time before the police were on his trail. Merrett, alias Chesney, had a criminal record which identified him all over Europe. He shot himself because he recognized that his number was up.

At the age of seventeen and a half, on March 17, 1926, he had shot his mother through the side of the head. His reason was that he had been forging her signature on cheques, and was afraid that he was going to be found out. His history has become famous for the fact that, when he was tried in Edinburgh for matricide, the Scottish jury of ten men and five women brought in a majority verdict of 'Not proven.' He was merely sent to prison for twelve months for uttering forged cheques.

In his autobiography, Sir Sydney Smith, Emeritus Professor of Forensic Medicine at Edinburgh University, expresses the feeling that the verdict aroused among experts at the time:

> The slackness of the police and the credit given to the misleading evidence of Spilsbury and Churchill, who had made a mistake and were too stubborn to admit it, allowed Merrett to live — and to kill again. A worthless life was saved, and two innocent women were thereby condemned to die.

In retrospect, no one can fairly disagree with Sir Sydney's summing up of the case, except perhaps with the justice of his comment that Churchill and Spilsbury 'made a mistake and were too stubborn to admit it.' That opinion rests on what I believe to be a delicate and still unresolved point of professional conduct — the question as to how far the expert witness, especially when he appears for the defence, should volunteer evidence of value to the other side.

Churchill always insisted that he gave his evidence irrespective of whether it helped the prosecution or the defence. He refused on principle to support Marshall Hall's plea in the Green Bicycle Case. On several occasions, when he was called for the Crown, his evidence destroyed the Crown's case. During the Merrett trial, when a newspaper reporter asked him, 'Do you think the prisoner is guilty?' he replied: 'I don't know. I am only interested in the firearms side of the case.'

With the knowledge that Merrett was certainly guilty, it is interesting to imagine oneself as a juryman in the trial before the Lord Justice-Clerk (Lord Alness) which began at Edinburgh on February 1, 1927, when what had previously passed as a suicide case had been transformed into a charge of murder.

★ ★ ★

It is so perilously easy to be wise after the event that, on the facts of the case, one wonders that the jury were ever in doubt. The defence made scarcely an effort to clear Merrett of the charge that he had forged his mother's signature on her cheques. The evidence was overwhelming that, while he was supposed to be a student at Edinburgh

216

University, he was playing the Casanova at cheap dance halls. He had purchased for £1 15s, after obtaining a firearms' certificate from the police (on what grounds heaven knows), a .25 automatic pistol of Spanish make with fifty rounds of ammunition from Hardy Brothers in Princes Street. He was alone in the room with his mother when she was shot. He had the motive, the opportunity, and the means. The case rested on whether it could be proved, without possibility of doubt, that he did indeed shoot his mother, and that she didn't shoot herself.

Merrett had the inestimable advantage as a murderer that he didn't run away. When he shot his mother, through the lobe of her ear shortly after breakfast, he reported the event to the daily maid. When the police came they never questioned that it was a case of attempted suicide. Poor Mrs Merrett was detained at the Royal Infirmary, Edinburgh, in a cell with barred windows in the shadow that on her discharge arrangements would be made for taking her into custody for attempted *felo de se*.

With a bullet in her head, she lived astonishingly for a fortnight. She told her nurses that she had heard 'a kind of explosion.' She was surprised that a pistol was involved. 'Did Donald do it?' she asked. 'He is such a naughty boy.' Before he shot her she remembered that she said: 'Go away, Donald, and don't annoy me.' Up to her death she never accused him. At the trial the judge described the failure of the police to take a dying deposition from her as 'an almost criminal neglect of an obvious and imperative duty.'

From the beginning the police and the doctors were at fault. The police, believing that it was a suicide case, failed to make a conclusive record of the position of the weapon and the body, and produced a witness in the daily maid who contradicted her story twice. Professor Harvey Littlejohn, the eminent pathologist of Edinburgh University, concluded from the post-mortem examination that the case was consistent with suicide. It was only later that it was discovered that Mrs Merrett's son had 'uttered as genuine' twenty-nine cheques upon her bank account. Only then was he charged with murder and forgery.

Mrs Merrett believed that her husband, who had deserted her many years earlier, was dead. It emerged in the trial that he wasn't. There is reason to suppose that John Alfred

Merrett had associations with the Secret Service.[1] Otherwise, it is difficult to understand how such a formidable, expensive, and determined defence was organised on his son's behalf. Mr Craigie M. Aitchison, KC, was briefed to represent him. Even more remarkable, Bernard Spilsbury, who had never appeared in any case except for the Crown, and Churchill, who himself normally gave evidence for the Director of Public Prosecutions, were called for Merrett's defence. It is one of those trials, like Mrs Barney's five years later, in which the circumstances are charged with question-marks.

Churchill himself said that he had never worked so hard on any case in which he had been called: 'I took my wife with me to Edinburgh during the ten days I was there with the idea of making some visits to friends after Court hours, but counsel for the defence was indefatigable. We had

---

[1] Major Hugh B. C. Pollard writes: 'Informed gossip at the time held that Merrett's father was a rather important figure in Intelligence in South America; not necessarily under the same name. Mrs Merrett was dead and 'reasons of State' are sometimes more important than the conviction of a horrible adolescent.'

conferences each evening after dinner in which we went right through the transcript of the shorthand notes of the day's proceedings and prepared the next day's work as well.'

The trial settled into a conflict between experts; and nine of them were called. The choice was to decide whether the shot which killed Mrs Merrett was sufficiently close to be self-inflicted or at a range sufficiently far to establish that the gun must have been fired by her son. It is important to remember that, at the time, the prejudice of the jury was in favour of suicide; and that the men and women on it were reluctant to convict a youth of the unnatural crime of murdering his own mother. Further, the evidence for the prosecution was inconclusive.

Professor Harvey Littlejohn, the chief medical witness for the Crown, had asserted after the post-mortem examination in April 1926 that:

> there is nothing to indicate the distance at which the discharge of the weapon took place, whether from a few inches or a greater distance. So far as the position of the wound is concerned, the case is consistent with suicide. There is some

difficulty in attributing it to accident, although such a view cannot wholly be excluded.

When Sir Sydney Smith suggested to him that it was murder Professor Littlejohn, after various experiments, made a new report with a different conclusion, over a month after Merrett had been charged with the murder of his mother. Counsel for the defence didn't let him forget that he had changed his mind.

In fact, there wasn't a large difference in the factual evidence, although there was an important difference in conclusion, given by the experts on both sides. Merrett would have hanged if it could have been established that the bullet which killed his mother was fired at more than three inches' range. At a lesser range there was a reasonable doubt as between suicide and murder. It was that matter of inches which saved Merrett's neck.

Not the least difficulty of the nine experts on both sides was that there was no evidence of scorching or tattooing — or if there had been it had been swabbed away — round the wound through the lobe of Mrs Merrett's ear. If evidence of scorching from the powder in the cartridge could have been established it would have materially assisted the case for the defence because it would have shown that the pistol was fired from a range close enough to admit that the possibility of suicide couldn't be discounted.

The experts for the prosecution, led by Professor Harvey Littlejohn, waffled. Littlejohn, after reporting that the case was 'consistent with suicide,' changed his mind and made his second report that there was no indication of blackening or tattooing by ingrained particles of powder to suggest a near shot; 'i.e. within 3″ of head.' Professor Glaister said in evidence: 'I am unable to exclude absolutely the production of such a wound as in this case by self-infliction.' Mr McNaughten, the Edinburgh gunmaker, stated that the explosive in the pistol was 'a modified form of cordite, called smokeless powder, which caused less discolouration than gunpowder.'

By contrast, Churchill and Spilsbury commanded the court. Sir Sydney Smith, who had no love for either of them, makes in his autobiography a notable back-handed compliment:

To counter Littlejohn's expert evidence they put up Sir Bernard Spilsbury, the Home Office pathologist, who was very brilliant and very famous, but fallible like the rest of us — and very, very

222

obstinate. In England, where he always appeared for the Crown, many murderers were justly convicted on his evidence. Now he was making one of his rare appearances for the defence. With him was Robert Churchill, often described as the expert on ballistics. Robert Churchill was famous, too, and I am sure he was an excellent gunsmith. He also was stubborn and dogmatic. He and Spilsbury often appeared together in shooting cases, and they were indeed a formidable team — terrifying when they made a mistake, as they did here.

But did they? Merrett, as subsequent events proved, was guilty. But Spilsbury and Churchill were called to show that it was *possible*, on the existing evidence, that Mrs Merrett committed suicide. At the time nobody except Merrett himself knew any more. In that knowledge it is difficult to accept that Churchill's and Spilsbury's evidence was 'mistaken.' Churchill's own opinion was that the other side made a mess of the case. The prosecution insisted that it was impossible for Mrs Merrett's wound to have been self-inflicted, although their own expert witnesses were uncertain in the matter.

Churchill and Spilsbury did no more than demonstrate that suicide was, in fact, a possibility.

Together they had worked hard on the case. Churchill maintained that the absence of scorching or blackening round Mrs Merrett's wound wasn't significant. 'Smokeless powder will mark paper or cardboard but it will not indelibly mark skin. Experiments with animal skin are not satisfactory; it doesn't respond like live human flesh. Superficial powder blackening round a wound may be washed away by the flow of blood. This was especially true,' Churchill added, 'in the Merrett case where the weapon was a little .25 automatic pistol. The cartridge, with a two-grain charge of nitrocellulose powder, consumed itself within an inch of leaving the barrel. Our London experiments with a similar pistol confirmed this view.'

Bernard Spilsbury insisted on the experiment. When Churchill told him that shooting at inanimate targets would prove nothing Spilsbury sent the word round the London hospitals that he wanted a lump of human flesh. In due course the amputated leg of an elderly woman patient was provided. Wrapped in a brown-paper parcel, the two experts took the macabre object in the train to Churchill's shooting grounds in Kent. They hadn't got the pistol in the case, but they used a weapon of the same calibre and ammunition from the same shop that Merrett had bought his own gun. At varying distances, firing at the amputated leg, they established that there was no trace of a powder-mark on the skin.

Churchill himself wasn't entirely happy with the experiment. He said to me years later that, if it had been any other than Spilsbury, counsel would have challenged his evidence by pointing out that the reaction of dead flesh is quite different from living flesh. But Churchill himself was in no doubt that the evidence of the experiment, such as it was, was of no significance. Curiously enough, Professor Harvey Littlejohn, for the prosecution, had been experimenting with shots into human flesh himself.

Littlejohn, using Merrett's pistol, found that at three inches the automatic 'left very definite powder and burning marks round the wound in the skin area. Further, the discoloration on the skin couldn't be readily washed off.' Later Churchill and Spilsbury attended a demonstration in Edinburgh of test shots at white cardboard with the same pistol with similar results. Churchill believed that neither the results on cardboard on that occasion nor the dead flesh in his experiments with Spilsbury in London were conclusive.

He knew that Hugh Pollard, behind the scenes, had constructed ear membranes of a glycerine and gelatine substance which he had tested to see if any confidence could be reposed in the absence, or otherwise, of blackening. There was no decisive information to be drawn from that experiment either.

In his evidence Churchill described the scorching effect that a small automatic at close range would have on live human skin. But he advanced an explanation of Mrs Merrett's death, subsequently supported by Spilsbury, and the judge too, which transformed the case. Examining him, Mr Craigie Aitchison asked:

'Have you in your experience had a case of a suicidal wound behind the right ear?'

'Yes.'

'Was that the case of a man or woman?'

'The case of a woman.'

'Who shot herself behind the right ear?'

'Yes.'

'Was the weapon directed forwards or backwards?'

'Forwards.'

'Did it roughly correspond to the direction

of the wound in this case?'

'Yes, roughly.'

'And was that an undoubted case of suicide?'

'It was brought in as suicide.'

'It has been suggested, but I do not think persisted in, that, in order to get the weapon into such a position as to produce a wound of the kind we have here, the hand would need to be put into a strained position. What do you say to that?'

'I say that it is quite possible to reproduce that wound without any movement of the arm at all — just a movement of the head. I teach shooting, and I find that women flinch from the discharge at first, by closing their eyes and by turning the head away from the discharge instinctively.'

'Does it come to this, that supposing the weapon were pointed at the side of the temple, an instinctive movement of the head, without any movement of the arm, might get the pistol into the position that would give you the direction we have in this case?'

'You could reproduce this wound exactly by doing that.'

'In your view, can the angle be easily accounted for on the view that the pistol was pointed at the temple, but there was an instinctive aversion of the head at the moment the trigger was pulled?'

'It is possible to reproduce this wound in that way.'

'And, if this was a case of suicide, would you, from your experience of instinctive movements of the head when firearms are fired, think it a likely thing to occur?'

'Yes. I have also considered the wound from the point of view of accident.'

'In your view, could a wound of this kind, having regard to all the facts, direction and so on, have been accidentally caused?'

'I could reproduce that wound by holding the pistol with the thumb on the trigger-guard and the fingers of the hand at the butt of the pistol.'

'Assume that Mrs Merrett — she seeing the pistol in the bureau — had picked it up in that position, and assuming that she over-balanced and fell, is there any difficulty at all in getting an accidental discharge that would produce a wound in the head such as you find here?'

'No.'

Churchill demonstrated his theory by putting his thumb on the trigger, with the butt of the pistol in the palm of the hand, and jarring the back of the hand on the ledge of the witness-box, the muzzle being pointed towards the head and the face averted from the pistol.

'Accordingly, are the facts in your view consistent with accident?'

'Accident is possible.'

'Similarly, supposing that, having lost her balance at the moment the pistol was in her hand, she instinctively raised her hand to her head to protect her head in the fall, is there any difficulty in getting the pistol into a position that is consistent with accident?'

'There is no difficulty in getting the pistol into position, but I should not expect it to happen that way. I think I have given the two most likely ways that this could happen. I think the most likely way is to pick the pistol up with the thumb on the trigger guard and to fall on it.'

'Which might happen if Mrs Merrett had her chair tilted up at the time?'

'It is possible to reproduce the wound in that way.'

'Is it in accordance with your knowledge and experience of firearms that accidents occur which it is sometimes impossible to explain?'

'It is impossible to explain some of them.'

'In the case of gunshot wounds where you are using a gun — I mean suicidal wounds where you are using a gun — where do you usually find them, or where do you often find them?'

'Usually in the mouth.'

'Where you have a suicidal wound from a long-barrelled revolver, where do you frequently find them?'

'Usually in the temple. I am saying usually, because sometimes they are in the mouth.'

'But when you find a wound inflicted with a short-barrelled firearm, such as the automatic pistol you hold in your hand, where do you usually find them?'

'Usually in the side of the head. A shotgun, on account of its very long barrel, naturally can only be placed in the mouth. A long-barrelled revolver can be placed in the mouth, because there is something you can put in; and also it can be put, on account of its length, at the side of the head. But with an automatic pistol, such as I have in my hand, it is natural to do it at the side.'

'Taking all the facts as you have them in this case, do you find anything in the position or the direction of the wound to exclude either suicide or accident?'

'No.'

He was cross-examined by the Lord Advocate:

'Take first of all your suggested possible method, that of suicide, which you have demonstrated, are you assuming that this is a woman who is not skilled in firing pistols?'

'A woman who is nervous of firearms, and I find that every woman is nervous at first.'

'Is it a very uncommon thing for a woman to commit suicide with a pistol?'

'I have had a few cases. Naturally, it is not common.'

'And still more uncommon for women who are ignorant of the use of such weapons?'

'I would say that.'

'Among these few cases, was there any one of a woman committing suicide with a pistol in the presence of a near relative, such as a son?'

'In one case a woman committed suicide for no apparent reason. The shot was behind the ear, and no action was taken against the husband, who was asleep in a chair alongside. That is the only case I can cite near to this.'

'Assuming that sitting in the chair Mrs Merrett put her elbow at the angle you have suggested, it would come in contact, or risk coming into contact, with the bureau. Does not that exclude the possibility of your theory?'

'No.'

'If it did come in contact, it would upset it. If there was a risk it would render it doubtful?'

'Yes.'

'Come now to your suggestion of accident. The only suggestion you make, as I understand, is that the thumb goes into the trigger guard with the hand grasping the butt of the pistol?'

'Yes.'

'But, surely, the person so grasping it must have known the pistol was there?'

'That is right.'

'You could not put any papers between, or the thumb would not go into the trigger guard, would it?'

'No.'

'Were you assuming that the pistol was picked up off the bureau?'

'I am simply assuming that the lady was sitting in the chair and was stretching out.'

'You do not know whether she needed to tip the chair or not in order to reach the pigeon-holes?'

'No.'

'Or whether it would be possible for her to tilt the chair?'

'I expect that in the case of accident she would have to tip the chair to fall.'

'Are you assuming that she is sitting at an angle to the bureau, with her back half towards it?'

'Yes, falling back on the right hand against the bureau.'

'The effect of that would be to jerk the pistol out of her hand, probably, would it not?'

'I am assuming that she falls on to the pistol.'

'You are assuming that she stretched towards the pigeon-hole to get the pistol out of it?'

'Yes.'

'Are you aware that there are some 20 inches between the pigeon-hole and the edge of the writing slab on the bureau?'

'No, I do not know.'

'So that the pit of her arm would be touching the writing slab as she reached for the pistol?'

'I do not know that.'

'That would rather affect the theory that you are putting forward?'

'It would, if the body were stopped by this bureau.'

'You made certain experiments in London. It was you who actually did the firing?'

'Yes.'

'Were those experiments made with a different pistol and different cartridges and gunpowder to those which we know were used in this case?'

'Yes, a pistol of similar make, of Spanish manufacture, and the ammunition supposedly of similar but of later make.'

'It was a different maker, was it not?'

'It was Nobel's ammunition. They are all one combine.'

'Do I understand that you experimented on both skin and cardboard in London and in Edinburgh?'

'Yes.'

'Did the powder used in London produce more of a yellowish colour and not so black as in Edinburgh?'

'The powder used in London produced more tattooing.'

'But was not the colour more of a yellowish tinge?'

'Slightly flame.'

'You would agree, in view of your experience, that the advisable thing in every case is to carry out tests with the actual weapon, and with as identical powder and ammunition as you can get?'

'Yes.'

'On the Sunday, 30th January, eight days ago, was it you who actually fired the pistol?'

'Yes.'

'Was the pistol in good working order?'

'Yes.'

He was re-examined by Mr Aitchison:

'You were asked whether you knew of any case in which a mother had shot herself in the presence of her son. You do recollect a case in which a wife shot herself in the presence of her husband?'

'Yes.'

'And there was a Home Office investigation?'

'Yes.'

'Was that established as a case of suicide?'

'Yes.'

'And did the investigations reveal any motive of any kind?'

'No motive.'

★　★　★

Churchill was followed into the box by Sir Bernard Spilsbury. Spilsbury added the opinion that women, through the lifelong habit of putting up their hair, had a great extension of the shoulder-joint and, as a consequence, it was possible to imagine that Mrs Merrett could hold a small pistol in a position to point it at the back of her skull. He insisted that her wound could not be considered as definitely inflicted by another person. Spilsbury said that he thought it was suicide.

The assuredness of the two expert witnesses for the defence undoubtedly carried the jury. The judge was equally impressed. In his summing up, in Scotland called 'the charge to the jury,' Lord Alness said that the chief objection suggested to the theory of suicide from the direction of the wound was that it would involve a constrained position of the arm on firing. 'Well, you will consider whether that objection was not met, or invalidated, by the exceptionally simple suggestion made by the London gun expert, Mr Churchill, that a sudden and instinctive aversion of the head by the person who was going to fire the pistol would naturally account for the position of the wound, without any constrained position of the arm.'

The jury brought in the middle verdict of 'Not Proven' on the murder charge. While Scottish law is often criticised in England, it meant exactly what it said. Merrett wasn't proved guilty, but the jury thought he was. Further, it is unarguable that Spilsbury and Churchill between them saved his unworthy neck, although Churchill himself gave all the credit to the counsel for the defence.

'Mr Craigie Aitchison, afterwards Lord Aitchison, was in my opinion the best cross-examiner I ever heard. The way he used the Scottish phrase 'come awa' with it' to a witness until the witness did indeed 'come awa' with it' was wonderful. I was very tickled when, in examination, he waved his fingers prettily at Sir Bernard Spilsbury and said, more phonetically than I can write it: 'Now tell me, Saint Berr-nard!' In court, it passed unnoticed.

'The book of the case in the 'Notable British Trials' series does not reveal the skill with which Craigie Aitchison conducted his defence, how he threw quick-fire questions at one witness until he had conceded his point; how he played with another, not so intelligent, until he had got the evidence he wanted. Craigie Aitchison and his junior got Merrett off. In that case, counsel was the Scottish Marshall Hall, Muir and Norman Birkett rolled into one.'

History has placed the blame for Merrett's acquittal firmly on the shoulders of Churchill and Spilsbury. It is undeniable that the evidence of the two best witnesses in the land influenced the judge and the jury. It is probably true that neither Spilsbury nor Churchill believed that Merrett was innocent. The heart of the affair is simply whether they thought, as they did, that Mrs Merrett's death could possibly have been caused by suicide or accident. It is a matter of conscience to decide whether it was right for Spilsbury and Churchill to advance the best argument that they could for the defence, or whether they should have refused to appear at all. Myself, I don't know the answer.

PICTURE A MURDERER

(Edwin Bush, UK 1961)

Richard Jackson

Identifying a suspect in a murder case can be a hazardous business. Witnesses are often confused, sometimes frightened, occasionally mistaken. But their ability to recall facial characteristics can be crucial. In the late 1950s, new techniques were developed to improve the likeness achieved by a combination of witness descriptions and artists' impressions. The first of these facial assembly techniques was known as 'Identikit'. Guided by an eye-witness, a skilled operator assembled transparencies of the suspect's key facial features into a two-dimensional composite. The picture could then be circulated by the police. In 1961, Edwin Bush became the first murder suspect in Britain to be brought to book by the Identikit method of compiling a picture of a suspect's face. Bush was arrested within four days of the Identikit's publication by a policeman on patrol. Richard Jackson (1902-75) was

238

assistant commissioner (CID) at New Scotland Yard. But by training and temperament he was a criminal lawyer rather than a policeman, and an excellent raconteur, a trait that endeared him to the press. He held and expressed trenchant views of a range of subjects, including the need for tough sentences for violent criminals and a detestation of liberal reformers. When he retired in 1963, Richard Jackson received a knighthood and wrote his memoirs, in which he recalled how the new-fangled Identikit technique resulted in the arrest and conviction of a killer.

'If this paper remains blue,' Sherlock Holmes told Watson, 'all is well. If it turns red, it means a man's life.' He dipped the litmus paper into a test tube and it flushed into a dull, dirty crimson . . .

Conan Doyle's stories may have had some influence in showing the police how science can be used as an aid to detection, and even more influence in leading the public to think of forensic science as a kind of magic. It is a very useful aid; it isn't a kind of magic. Criminals are caught by men, not by gadgets.

Forensic science has, of course, tremendously advanced since Sherlock Holmes's day, particularly in its ability to show, by matching minute particles of soil or dust or thread or cellulose, that a suspect must have been at the scene of the crime. As well as the laboratory techniques which support them, as it were, behind the lines, the police have acquired a number of gadgets to help both in their preventive and in their investigative work. Rapidly coming into use now are personal two-way radios carried by constables on the beat, hidden television cameras to keep a watch on vulnerable streets and markets and car parks, and an infra-red spotlight for use at night.

One device which we acquired during my period at the Yard caught the public imagination more than any other — the Identikit.

I first heard about it on July 30th, 1959. At a lunch that day in the Café Royal I met a huge genial giant of a man, called Pete Pitchess. He had been in the FBI and was now Sheriff of Los Angeles County. After lunch he came back to the Yard to see the Black Museum and the Information Room. When we were having a drink in my room afterwards, with a few senior officers whom I'd invited to meet him, he showed us a piece of equipment which had been invented by his Deputy, Hugh McDonald. It was a book of

240

interchangeable transparent flaps, each with a drawing of some part of a face — eyes, eyebrows, hairline, nose, mouth, and so on; rather like those books in which children put the head of a giraffe on to the body of a lion and the legs of an ostrich. With this range of possible parts, Pitchess said, a useful picture of a wanted man could be built up from the selection made by a witness who had seen him.

There was nothing new, of course, about constructing pictures from eyewitnesses' descriptions. As long ago as 1935, when I was prosecuting in the Grierson case, I was struck by what a good likeness the police drawing had been of the man who eventually appeared in the dock; it was a profile, I remember, with a hooked nose and glasses. But in Britain (contrary to the practice in some other countries) the artist didn't normally work with the witness; he merely followed a description which was handed to him. And a witness who is shown a completed drawing is too apt to accept it, whereas an Identikit picture can be continually altered until the witness really does feel satisfied that it represents the face he saw.

I showed the Identikit to the Commissioner, and we both expressed interest in the possibility of acquiring it. A week or so later I received a letter from the American company which manufactured the equipment. (If the company had been British I dare say I should never have heard any more about it, not for months or years anyway.) Pitchess had told them of our interest, they said; they were willing to consider leasing it to us, and they invited us to send an officer to California for a course of training. I replied that I couldn't spare a man. There was further correspondence, during which they asked me, among other things, for a list of every police force in Britain with more than a hundred officers. I sent it to them. They pondered on the size of the potential market, and, the following spring, offered to send their representative to Scotland Yard, to run a course of instruction here.

After clearing this proposal with the Commissioner, the Receiver, and the Home Office I circulated it to all provincial forces through the Chief Officers Association and the Chief Constables of Scotland Association. The response was gratifying. We finally arranged a three-day course for the beginning of March 1961.

The class consisted of thirty-one officers — ten detective sergeants from the Metropolitan Police, twenty provincial officers, and one officer from the United States Air Force. Superintendent Du Rose of C1 was in charge, and the instruction was given by Deputy Sheriff Hugh McDonald himself, who proved to be extremely good.

The course ended on Friday, March 3rd. A detective sergeant from 'H' Division went back to his duties next day, and, using the Identikit, was immediately able to catch three men who had committed a robbery. But a more serious crime had been reported in 'E' Division.

At 12.15 p.m. that Friday, before the Identikit course was even ended, I heard that a woman had been found stabbed to death in an antique shop in Cecil Court, off the Charing Cross Road. The body had been discovered by the proprietor, Louis Meier. A wireless car from Bow Street arrived, and the officers found the dead woman lying on her back with an antique dagger stuck in her breast and another in her neck.

She was Mrs Elsie May Batten, and she had been an assistant in the shop. The daggers, which had evidently been taken from the stock, still had their price tickets on them.

At 12.30 Detective Superintendent Pollard arrived. In those first few hours his chances of success seemed steadily to dwindle. There was no reason to suppose — and, since the weapons were clearly impromptu, it seemed unlikely — that Mrs Batten had been killed by a personal enemy; nor had she been sexually assaulted. Robbery was the likeliest motive, but her handbag and the box used as a till both appeared to be untouched; Mr Meier couldn't say if anything had been removed from his stock. Local inquiries elicited nothing. A hairdresser opposite had seen Mrs Batten open the shop at 9.15, but since then nobody had been observed going in or out. The only clue Pollard found was a piece of wood under the dead woman's legs, bearing the impression of a heel and faint sole marks.

When the pathologist, Dr Keith Simpson, arrived halfway through the afternoon he found a third dagger underneath the body and a third stab wound in the back. He said the woman had also been struck on the head with a heavy stone ornament, and he confirmed that there had been no sexual interference.

Then things began to move. A fifteen-year-old boy, an apprentice sign-writer, was brought to the police by his uncle. The boy had told his uncle, and now told us, that he had gone into Meier's shop at about half-past eleven that morning to buy a billiard cue, and had seen what he thought was a dummy lying on the floor at the back. When he realized it was a woman he assumed she had fainted — and promptly left the shop. Which doesn't seem a very chivalrous act. Perhaps he was a timid boy.

Meanwhile Meier recalled that a young man who said he was half-Indian and half-English had been in the shop during Mrs Batten's lunch hour on the previous day. This Eurasian had spent some time examining the antique daggers, but had left without buying anything. He had returned later, accompanied by a girl, and asked the price of a dress sword. Mrs Batten had remarked to Meier afterwards that it was odd for a man so poorly dressed to be interested in a sword costing £15. Meier gave us a description of the young man, and said he thought that he would be able to recognize him. All he could remember about the girl was that she looked somewhere between seventeen and twenty, and was fair-haired. There were several dress swords in the shop, and he couldn't say if any of them were missing.

A team of twenty detectives, under Superintendent Pollard, began working their way through all the other antique shops and jewellers. But they found what they wanted, next morning, only a few yards away.

Opposite Meier's shop was a gunmaker.

His nineteen-year-old son had been alone there on the morning of the murder when, soon after 10 a.m., a young Indian walked in and tried to sell him a dress sword. The sword had been wrapped in a sheet of brown paper. When he was asked how much he wanted for it the Indian replied, 'I paid fifteen pounds, but I'll take ten.' The gunmaker's son rightly thought this a suspicious remark. He asked the Indian to come back at 11.15, when his father would be in. The Indian agreed and left the sword, but never returned.

The gunmaker himself now added a piece of information. A dark young man — he couldn't remember much else about his looks — had called at the shop on the previous afternoon, and asked, 'Do you buy swords?' The gunmaker said he might, but he would need to see the article. The young man replied that this sword had an engraving on it, and he promised to bring it in.

So we now had the sword. It was immediately identified by another woman who worked part-time in Meier's shop, and who remembered having shown it to a customer the week before. The brown paper had gone, having been used to wrap up a pair of gun-barrels, but Pollard's men traced it to a customer in Kilburn, and sent it, together with the sword, to the fingerprint department at the Yard.

Meier and the gunmaker's son were each able to give a clear and detailed description of the young Eurasian; so, less than twenty-four hours after the course had ended, we had an ideal opportunity for giving Identikit a trial run. On March 4th one of the officers who had been on the course, Detective Sergeant Dagg, interviewed Meier and the gunmaker's son — separately — and built up pictures matching the descriptions they gave him. The two pictures proved strikingly similar, except for one detail: the hair style was quite different.

I was shown photographs of these two Identikit reconstructions. They looked good enough to be useful and close enough to one another not to cause confusion. I decided that not only should they both be circulated to all police forces, but they should also be published in the Press and shown on television. At the same time we released Meier's much vaguer description of the girl.

Four days later, at 1.40 p.m., a certain PC Cole was on duty in Old Compton Street, Soho, when he spotted a young man who seemed to match the picture. And the young man was accompanied by a girl of about seventeen with blonde hair. Cole stopped them, and told the man that he fitted the description of someone wanted for questioning in connection with the Cecil Court murder.

'Yes, I saw the photo in the paper,' said the young man casually. 'It did look a bit like me.'

The accent — Cockney, not Peter Sellers-type Indian — also matched the police circulation. Cole asked them both to come with him to the police station.

'I'd rather not,' said the man. 'We're going to buy a ring.'

Cole insisted, and, since this was a murder case, he took no chances. He searched the man, there and then. Finding no weapons, he marched the couple off towards a police telephone box in Cambridge Circus. An off-duty constable in civilian clothes saw what was happening and telephoned for a police car while Cole stood guard over his prisoners. Both the man and the girl repeatedly asked to be allowed to go; they were in a hurry, they said. Which merely intensified Cole's suspicions. Then a car arrived and whisked them away to Bow Street.

The young man was half-Indian, half-English, and gave his name as Edwin Bush. He was just twenty-one years old. As soon as he arrived at Bow Street impressions were taken of the soles and heels of his shoes.

While these were being compared with the marks found under the body Pollard questioned the girl.

She was seventeen and had known Bush for about two months, and had come into the West End with him that day to choose an engagement ring. As it was also his twenty-first birthday, they were going to have a double celebration at an Indian restaurant.

She denied ever having been to the antique shop in Cecil Court, and, oddly enough, she was telling the truth. As we discovered later, the girl who had accompanied Bush was his sister, aged eighteen and not blonde at all but very dark. It was sheer luck that, because Meier wrongly thought she had been fair, the description happened to fit the couple whom Cole picked out from the crowd in Old Compton Street.

While Pollard questioned the girl, detectives called at Bush's home. His mother said he had left the house at 7.30 am on March 3rd, presumably for work. When in due course Pollard asked him about his movements on March 3rd he immediately said that he had spent the whole of that morning at home with his mother. The shoe-prints matched.

Pollard told the duty officer at Bow Street that he wanted to hold an identification parade. This was easier said than done, since it involved collecting nine men of similar age and colour who could speak English without a foreign accent. Eventually a group was assembled, and the parade was held at 10.25 p.m. Meier walked down the line first. He stood for some time in front of Bush, then said, 'I'm not positive, but I think this is the man.' The gunmaker's son was brought in. He picked Bush with no hesitation at all.

Pollard then charged Edwin Bush with the murder of Mrs Batten. After a moment's silence Bush said, 'The girl is nothing to do with it. I did it alone.' And he went on to make a statement admitting that he had killed Mrs Batten in order to steal the sword. Just to clinch matters, there was blood on some of his clothes, and his palm-print and two of his fingerprints were found on the brown paper in which the sword had been wrapped.

When he came up for trial at the Old Bailey in May he pleaded not guilty to capital murder. He now said that he killed Mrs Batten, not to get the sword, but after she had made an offensive remark about the colour of his skin. Cross-examined by Mervyn Griffith-Jones, Bush didn't deny that he had in fact stolen the sword.

'You admit that you went into the shop in order to steal it, and admit that having stolen it you killed the lady with these three daggers?'

'Yes, sir.'

'You lost your temper simply because she passed the remark, 'You niggers are all the same, you come in and never buy anything'?'

'Yes, sir.'

In his summing up the judge instructed the jury that, if they believed this was the true cause of Bush's attack on Mrs Batten, they ought not to convict him of capital murder. They didn't believe it. After two hours' deliberation they found him guilty — which, the judge said afterwards, was the only possible verdict. Bush was hanged.

The result was a great deal of publicity for Identikit. The newspapers hailed it as a marvellous new aid to criminal investigation; and, sure as a Pavlovian reflex, some people expressed alarm at this new danger to civil liberties. How risky it would be, they said, to use composite pictures as evidence against an accused man! No one, of course, had ever suggested using them as evidence. If an arrest was made as a result of circulating an Identikit picture the witnesses would then have to identify the suspect in the ordinary way. 'If hopes were dupes, fears may be liars' — and *vice versa*. The apprehensions about Identikit were wholly unjustified, and the enthusiasm too was exaggerated. Identikit is simply a way — one way among several — of fixing, illustrating, and making permanent a witness's recollection, so as to help in the hunt for a wanted man when no photograph is available.

Its spectacular success in the Batten case proved a considerable embarrassment. Too much was then expected of it. As people saw more Identikit pictures, enthusiasm turned to ridicule. How odd, they said, that all wanted men should look just the same! But to policemen they don't look just the same; Identikit puts into visible form what a police description is supposed to provide — a catalogue of the few distinguishing marks which divide the wanted face from all the other human faces.

In his report to me after the course Superintendent Du Rose pointed out that one of the advantages, if Identikit were widely adopted, would be that a telephone call to a central index — the Criminal Record Office, perhaps — could by using a code of numbers and figures pass a likeness to other forces without any need to transmit the actual picture. It could be useful internationally, he suggested; and he arranged a demonstration for the Chief Superintendents of C1, which includes the Interpol Office, C9, and the

Criminal Record Office. Identikit requires trained operators, and he recommended that a phased scheme for its introduction should be adopted as soon as possible.

The arrangement we eventually made was that the apparatus itself remained the property of the American company, which would lease the sets to the forces which wanted them. The Receiver of the Metropolitan Police District agreed to act as the hiring agent for all British forces. Whereupon we immediately ran into a bureaucratic snag. We became liable for import dues, assessed by the Customs at an exorbitant figure. Not without difficulty, we obtained special exemption.

The possibility of using Identikit internationally was debated at length during the Interpol General Assembly in 1962. I realized then for the first time how many comparable systems were already in use. The Canadians, for example, had been using cut-up photographs of their own criminals for years; and there were several rival systems in the States. Advocates of these other systems objected to the use of the word 'Identikit' as though it were a generic, instead of a brand, name. The Assembly did not, in the end, recommend its international adoption, chiefly because it wasn't applicable at the moment to non-Caucasian faces.

That anyone could genuinely have objected, on principle, to the use of Identikit remains, to me, a great puzzle — or, at least, an example of the attitude of mind which is incorrigibly and irrationally suspicious of the police. British courts and our rules of evidence provide the most scrupulous protection for the accused. To extend this proper care and start complaining that the police weren't 'sporting' in the way they acquired the evidence is to tilt the whole balance of the law in favour of criminals, who aren't 'sporting' at all. In some ways the Americans have gone even further in this direction than we have, declaring inadmissible any evidence, however damning, which wasn't acquired in strict accordance with the rules — with the ludicrous result that confessed murderers have had to be released because their confessions weren't taken in quite the proper form.

Telephone-tapping is another example. On both sides of the Atlantic this aid to investigation has roused strongly hostile feelings and has now been forbidden except in very special circumstances. The Metropolitan Police are allowed to intercept telephone calls only on the signed authority of the Secretary of State after application has been made by the Assistant Commissioner. Such nice regard for privacy no doubt does us credit, but is it really necessary? Innocent people have much more to fear from the unimpeded activities of criminals than from the remote possibility that the privacy of their telephone calls might one day be unobtrusively infringed by the police — an infringement far less embarrassing to their domestic secrets than the crossed lines which our beloved telephone system is for ever mischievously providing.

THE BITER BIT

(Gordon Hay, 1968)

George Saunders

The case of teenager Gordon Hay was remarkable because he was convicted on the evidence of the teeth-marks found on the body of his victim. Expert medical evidence clearly showed that the characteristics of the bite-marks were consistent in every detail with a dental impression taken from Hay. The trial judge, Lord Grant, described forensic dentistry as a relatively new science, 'but there must, of course, always be a first time.' George Saunders (1923–95) reported Hay's trial for The Scotsman, the newspaper on which he worked as law reporter for some thirty years. He included this account in a collection of Scottish cases published shortly after his retirement in 1991.

The science of forensic odontology was still in its infancy in March 1968 when Scottish legal history was made by the conviction of an eighteen-year-old approved schoolboy,

Gordon Hay, known as 'Gags', for the murder of a fifteen-year-old Biggar schoolgirl, Linda Peacock. The successful use of odontology to identify Hay as the murderer by the bite mark he left on the young girl's breast was hailed as 'a forensic triumph.' Scottish courts had always been slow to accept the latest advances in science but, surprisingly, showed a new receptiveness on this occasion to careful scientific evidence in what became a classic case of circumstantial evidence.

Even the presiding judge, Lord Grant, the late Lord Justice Clerk of Scotland, described the case as 'unique, difficult and puzzling.'

The eminent pathologist, Professor Keith Simpson, then head of the Department of Forensic Medicine at Guy's Hospital, London, and leading expert on odontology, gave evidence at the trial. He had the highest praise for the Scottish team, who produced crucial evidence and showed infinite patience and attention to detail. They produced, he said, the finest 'bite mark' photography and dentition-matching that had yet been brought to court.

Both the Scottish experts, Detective-Inspector Osborne Butler and Dr Warren Harvey, who later became honorary consultant Forensic Odontologist to the Glasgow

Police, were aware that their work on the case was vital. The only proof of the murderer's identity, their evidence survived a most searching cross-examination at the trial.

Linda Peacock, who was only 5ft 1in tall, was the youngest of eight children. She was a bright and lively girl, interested in ponies, records and, naturally at her age, boys. She spent the afternoon of Sunday, 6 August 1967 at a farm busy with her favourite pastime, exercising ponies.

Linda then spent the evening in the Lanarkshire market town of Biggar. Normally, she would have gone to her sister's home in Main Street to wait for one of her brothers to take her home.

But, on that fateful evening, her sister was on holiday. Linda set off to walk more than a mile to her home at Swaire Cottage. She was last seen talking to friends in the town about 9.30 p.m. Next morning, she was found strangled under a yew tree in St Mary's Cemetery, only 269 yards away from where she was last seen alive. The police said there were sadistic touches to the murder and a massive manhunt began. The cemetery in unlit Carwood Road was screened from the narrow road by a 5-foot-high wall. It was not locked at night and was often used by courting couples.

The murder hunt was led by Detective Chief Superintendent William Muncie, the head of Lanarkshire CID who had successfully led investigations into fifty murders, including those committed by mass murderer, Peter Manuel. He later became Assistant Chief Constable of Strathclyde before his well-earned retirement. Muncie's patience, clever reasoning and dogged determination had made him a legend in the force.

More than 100 officers from the Lanarkshire force and the Regional Crime Squad began a house-to-house search in the vicinity immediately after Linda was found. Tracker dogs were used in the surrounding fields and every male over fourteen in the area was interviewed. A young couple had been seen on the road near the cemetery at about 10.15 p.m., just after Linda, on her own, was seen by two men who knew her and waved to her as they drove home. A woman told the police she heard a scream coming from the cemetery late on the Sunday evening.

Police began compiling reports on the movements of inmates and ex-inmates of nearby Loaningdale Approved School. The small town itself was in the grip of fear lest the killer would strike again. A petition calling for the return of capital punishment was signed by 20,000 people.

Nine days after the crime, the police returned to the scene of the murder to comb the area inch-by-inch. The bereaved parents, George Peacock, a retired electrician, and his wife, Mary, made an impassioned plea to the public for information.

But the investigation into their daughter's death would prove to be a slow and painstaking forensic exercise, and Hay would not be arrested and charged with the murder until 110 days after the crime. The police interviewed more than 300 people, drawing up a short list of 29 who could possibly have been involved. All of the short-listed individuals agreed to dental impressions being taken. After these were compared with transparencies of the bite marks on the girl's breast, the list was reduced to five.

Second impressions were then taken of these five. Six weeks after the murder, the team of four dental experts told the authorities they had eliminated everyone on the list except for No 11. It was only at this stage that it was revealed to them, in confidence, that No 11 was in fact Gordon Hay.

A further impression was still required in order for the dental experts to be absolutely certain. The Crown then took the unique step of applying to Sheriff-Substitute Gordon

Gillies, QC at Lanark for a warrant to authorise a third impression of Hay's teeth. The warrant was granted.

Hay, by then, was the principal suspect but had not yet been arrested. For this reason, the legality of taking a third impression of his teeth would be fiercely contested at his trial.

Largely on the strength of the odontological evidence, Hay was charged with the murder of Linda Peacock. Appearing at a pleading diet at Lanark, he lodged a special defence of alibi. When his trial opened in the High Court in Edinburgh on Monday, 26 February 1968, before a jury of six women and nine men, the Crown listed 105 witnesses, including Professor Simpson and other dental and medical experts.

Hay pleaded not guilty to murdering Linda by striking her on the head with an instrument, biting her on the breast, tying a ligature round her wrist and her neck and strangling her. His special defence of alibi claimed that between 9 p.m. and midnight, when the crime was alleged to have been committed, he was in the approved school.

Prosecuting for the Crown was Mr Ewan Stewart, QC, then Solicitor-General for Scotland who had already established a reputation as a terrier of a prosecutor — probably the best prosecutor in Scotland for many years. His patient and sometimes aggressive cross-examinations had proved the downfall of many criminals. He was assisted by Mr Hugh Morton (later Lord Morton of Shuna, a judge in the Court of Session). For the defence there was an equally tenacious Stewart, Mr Ian Stewart, QC (later Lord Allanbridge), who was assisted by Mr James Law. Their battle over the medical evidence was to prove the highlight of the trial.

Lord Grant immediately ruled that no witnesses under seventeen should be named, adding that inmates of the approved school who were over seventeen should be treated in the same way.

Five local girls, all aged 15 or 16, told the court that girls had dates with boys from the school and that a pre-arranged signal — an owl hoot — was used to attract the attention of the boys when they were not meant to be out of the school. The boys, they said, got out of the school through the gymnasium.

One girl said Linda had a boyfriend in the school but he had left. Another girl recalled Linda speaking to Hay and another boy on Saturday, 5 August 1967 — the day before she was murdered — at a fun fair at Biggar.

The girls all said the boys at the school could come and go as they pleased, especially at weekends. One girl said she met boys from the school at the pictures on Saturday nights and went to dances at the school.

A sixteen-year-old boy who was a pupil at the school at the time said he was with Hay when they met Linda at the fun fair. Linda spoke to the boy but he walked on. Hay stayed behind, but his schoolmate did not know if he said anything to Linda. Afterwards, however, Hay told him he would not mind a night with her. Hay's schoolmate also described how some of the boys from the school had attended a camp at Montrose. After a beach barbecue on Friday, 4 August, the night before they returned, he saw one of the boys pick up a metal hook on the beach. On the evening of Linda's murder, at about 9 p.m. he saw Hay wearing pyjamas, a dressing gown and boots in his dormitory. He did not see Hay again that night.

But a fifteen-year-old boy who was also a pupil at the time said that when, after the murder, the police arrived at the school, Hay told him something like, 'We were in the dorm all last night'. He understood that this was what he was to tell the police, although it was not true.

Mr Ewan Stewart asked, 'Were you invited by Hay to tell a lie?' The boy replied, 'That was what it sounded like but I wasn't sure.'

The boy remembered Hay going to the

toilet in his pyjamas. Afterwards he fell asleep and woke up with the wireless playing. He did not know how long he had been asleep.

Cross-examined by Mr Ian Stewart, the boy said he had tried to get a date with Linda but failed. He also had written letters to her. Because of this he was a little bit worried. The police took away his clothes as well as those of Hay.

Two separate witnesses recalled hearing a scream from the cemetery about 10 p.m. A farmer's wife testified that she saw a couple standing in the cemetery, and had remarked to her husband that she had heard of courting couples in many places but not in a churchyard. A local farmer who had known Linda all her life stated that while passing Carwood Road in his van he had seen Linda. He had dogs in the back of his van and could not offer anyone in good clothes a lift; otherwise, he would have picked her up and taken her home.

Linda's father testified that on the day before her murder his daughter went to Huntfield to help with exercising ponies, returning home at about 4 p.m. The following day, Linda again went to Huntfield. He and his wife spent the day in Carluke. When they returned they found that their daughter was not at home. Worried, they contacted the police and a full-scale search began. Two constables found their daughter's body in the cemetery at 6.40 a.m.

She was lying partly under a yew tree beside a grave. A purse was near her head. There were bloodstains on the grass and blood on her head and cheek. A piece of string was found hanging from a nearby tree. Linda was lying on her back and her clothing was displaced. There was a deep weal round her neck which had broken the skin. Her anorak was bunched up under her head.

Detective-Sgt John Paton, who photographed the body, said there was bruising on the girl's breast which looked like bite marks. A doctor who examined the body said she was fully clothed but her upper garments had been drawn up, exposing the upper part of her body. Her lower garments were also drawn up. It appeared that a cord or string had been tightly tied round her neck.

Bank manager, Thomas Aitken, testified that while driving home he saw a young couple in his headlights near the cemetery. At home, he put on the television and heard Dickie Henderson introducing Frank Sinatra, Jun. on the *Blackpool Show*. He was later taken to Scottish Television's Glasgow studio where he saw a re-run of the programme, using a stop-watch to indicate the precise moment he first saw the programme. It showed that he first saw the programme about 10.20 p.m. It took 20 minutes to drive from the point where he had seen the young couple.

On the second day of the trial, a fifteen-year-old boy from Fife said he saw Hay in pyjamas, dressing gown and boots on the night of the murder. Later he saw the dressing gown and pyjamas lying on Hay's bed in the dormitory they shared. He fell asleep and was awakened by the door slamming. Hay was there with all his clothes on. His face was dirty and there was dirt on the knees of his jeans. His hair was dishevelled.

Another boy, who slept in the same dormitory, recalled finding a metal fishhook on the beach at Montrose. He brought it back to the school and put it on top of a wardrobe. He showed the hook to Hay, who said something about using it for fighting in Biggar.

He saw Hay that night taking part in a whist drive. Later, he watched *The Untouchables* on the television until about 9.55 p.m. He then went back to his dormitory but there was no one there. Because of something he had been told he looked for the hook but could not find it. The last time he saw it was the day before, when he had shown it to Hay.

He saw Hay's dressing gown and pyjamas on his bed. Feeling worried, and anxious to find the hook, he searched for Hay. He went through the dormitories, the games room, sitting room and dining room but Hay was not there.

Returning with another boy from his dormitory at about 10.15, he saw that Hay's dressing gown and pyjamas were still on his bed. Roughly ten minutes later, the two boys went to sleep.

The boy's most dramatic evidence described how he was woken up by the sound of the door slamming: 'I saw Gordon was there. He had his clothing on, light-coloured jeans and a school jersey. He had nothing on his feet but his socks. I don't think he knew I was awake.

'His face was dirty. His hair was as if he had been out in the wind. It was blown all over the place. It was just like he had been out working in the garden and sweating and he drew his hand across his face. His knees were a bit dirty, just like he had been kneeling down.'

Hay put on his pyjamas and washed at the sink. He was acting quite normally. Just as he was getting into bed a member of the staff turned out the lights and said 'Goodnight'.

Hay said 'Goodnight' back. Hay's room-mate awoke later when a car arrived bringing back their housemother. The three boys in the dormitory went to the window and spoke to her.

Hay's room-mate asked him where he had been; Hay denied he had been anywhere. The boy told Hay he had been looking for him; Hay asked him where he had looked and then said he had been in the bathroom. The next day, the boy found the metal hook in the bottom of the wardrobe and put it back on top.

When he was cross-examined, the boy admitted he had told lies to Hay's solicitor and to the police but said he was now telling the truth. Immediately after the murder he was not prepared to say anything that would implicate Hay but he later changed his mind.

A twenty-three-year-old student, William Bennett, who was acting as temporary housemaster at the school that night, had been in charge of Hay's dormitory. He told the court how Hay had won a prize that night at a whist drive. Not later than 10.35 p.m. Bennett went to the dormitory to turn out the lights. Hay had said 'Goodnight'. After 9.20 p.m. the staff were patrolling to see that the boys were getting ready for bed.

The deputy headmaster, Clifford Davies,

who was in charge that night, said he saw Hay in his dressing gown about 9.45 p.m. There was usually a check on the boys at 10 p.m. but there was no check that night because of the whist drive.

Three days after the crime, Hay was transferred to Rossie Farm Approved School, Montrose where, four days later, the police arrived to interview him. The headmaster, Mr John Henderson, insisted on being present as the police questioned Hay from 10 p.m. until 3.30 a.m. He was prepared to intervene, he told the court, if Hay were treated unfairly.

Asked if he had occasion to intervene, Mr Henderson replied 'The boot was on the other foot. The boy was impertinent to the police. He was truculent and aggressive.'

The boy was later taken away to Lanark and was brought back to Rossie Farm, the following evening. Hay claimed his nose had been injured but Henderson saw no sign of an injury. It was not unusual for approved schoolboys to hint that they had been mishandled by the police. Henderson found nothing to merit investigation.

Dr James Imrie, a lecturer in forensic medicine at Glasgow University who examined Linda Peacock's body at the cemetery and also carried out the post-mortem, told the court there was a ligature mark round her neck as well as bruising and the mark of a ligature on the left wrist. There was an area of bruising over the left breast. He thought it was caused by a bite.

There were white spots in the centre of the bruising on the breast. Asked what form of tooth would cause such a mark, Dr Imrie replied, 'A tooth with a hollow in its cutting edge.'

In the doctor's opinion, Linda had died between 10 p.m. and midnight. She was a virgin. On her left wrist there was blackening due to scorching as well as a blister. There were also two lacerations and bruising on her head. The doctor had found bloodstains on a grey shirt and trousers belonging to Hay. He said he had seen many bites in connection with sexual assaults and had tested for saliva with varying results. No saliva test was taken in this case. Even if it had been taken it might not have helped. There was no sign of wetness on the skin.

He had not considered the possibility of identifying the assailant as a result of the bite. If he had seen obvious teeth marks he would have considered it possible to identify the assailant. At the time, he said, they did not have it in mind to use the bite as a means of identification. If he had thought of this, he would have sent for a dentist to look at the breast.

When he was shown a metal hook, he agreed it could have caused the girl's injuries, although there were many other blunt instruments which could have done so.

On the third day of the trial, Lord Grant was accompanied on the Bench by Lords Walker and Milligan. The proceedings were interrupted by a three-hour debate on the question of whether evidence arising from the warrant to take impressions of Hay's teeth for the third time was admissible or not. Retiring for only five minutes following the debate, the judges returned to announce that the evidence was indeed admissible.

A week after Hay's conviction, Lord Grant issued a written judgment on this important ruling, which depended upon the judges' finding that the warrant authorizing the Crown to take impressions of Hay's teeth was valid. It had been argued that, since Hay was not present at the hearing of the petition for the warrant before the sheriff, it had been incompetently granted. Given that the Crown did not ask Hay's permission to take the third impression, the warrant would be illegal if it had not been competently granted. Had Hay been under arrest at the time, different considerations would have applied.

There was no doubt that a warrant to search premises was not illegal merely because the person concerned had not been apprehended or charged. The defence position, however, was that a search of premises was a very different matter from the possibly forcible invasion of the privacy of the person. Nor were there any reported cases of a warrant being granted to search the person.

Lord Grant said that although he was not persuaded that the difference was a matter of principle rather than degree a warrant to search the person should be granted only in very exceptional circumstances. Even if he was wrong in holding the warrant to be competent, he would have admitted the evidence, for in this case, by his committal to an approved school, Hay had largely ceased to be the master of his movements. In these very special circumstances, the Sheriff-Substitute was, in Lord Grant's opinion, justified in granting the warrant.

By the fourth day of the trial, the Crown had clearly shown that Hay was not around the school at the time of Linda Peacock's death. There was, however, little other evidence pointing to Hay as the assailant — until Professor Simpson electrified the court by confidently asserting that it was Hay's teeth which had caused the bite mark on the girl's breast.

Professor Simpson testified that he had thirty years' experience in forensic medicine and was consultant to New Scotland Yard. He had no dental qualifications but he had lectured all over the world on forensic odontology, had published articles on the subject, and was currently head of the Department of Forensic Medicine at London University: impressive credentials to support the crucial evidence he was about to give.

The marks on the girl's breast, Professor Simpson stated, were undoubtedly human bite marks. There were four marks which he regarded as quite characteristic of the points of pressure of teeth.

A firm hold had been made and the teeth had made a very distinct impression. There was some degree of suction; the bite must have been a painful one. In more than thirty years' practice the professor had seen many bite marks, both in his own cases and in others shown to him. He had never seen a bite mark with better defined detail than this.

It was accepted and orthodox practice to make transparencies and superimpose them over photographs of the injuries printed to the same scale in order to see to what extent exact matching took place. The methods in the Hay case followed the usual pattern.

Professor Simpson was shown photographs taken from plaster casts of Hay's teeth as well as transparencies superimposed on photographs of the bite marks. He told the court: 'I have looked at these with the greatest of care, as I commonly have to do with instruments of any kind in relation to marks on the skin.

'I see on this couple of superimposed transparencies a number of points of comparison, two of which, in my experience, are quite remarkable and quite unique.

'I would say that these two marks, in their position and in their character, and the other kind of mark which shows a scraping of the skin surface, for which I would require some explanation, are three quite exceptionally detailed marks.

'The presence of these three in this position and with those details would carry me a long way towards feeling that this was an exact comparison. I would be satisfied that this set of teeth — whichever it was — was the set that caused those marks'.

He was satisfied that Hay's teeth caused the bite marks on the girl's breast. Under cross-examination the professor said a saliva test was another test that could be applied in such cases. Some people excreted blood in their saliva and it might be possible to group the blood.

Mr Stewart said it was agreed by experts that it was easier to prove that bite marks were *not* caused by a particular suspect than to prove that they *were*. Professor Simpson replied that less trouble was entailed in excluding certain teeth. Others had to be studied more closely.

The court was told that in fingerprints sixteen points of comparison were required to conclusively identify a particular suspect. Asked if a similar claim could be made for forensic odontology, Professor Simpson replied that the number of points of comparison was not as great as in fingerprinting. There had been, for example, eight to ten points in an English case.

Detective Inspector Osborne Butler, of the Identification Bureau of Glasgow City Police, told the court that he went through the twenty casts of impressions of teeth taken from pupils and staff at Loaningdale and found that only No 11, belonging to Hay, fitted the marks found on the girl's breast. When he superimposed transparencies of Hay's teeth on the bite mark he found 'a demonstrable matching.' Hollows on the upper and lower canines, he said, corresponded with the bite mark.

During cross-examination, Detective Inspector Butler stated that the teeth marks were 'probably unique.' Asked if there would be any other teeth in Great Britain which could have made the marks, he replied, 'I would be surprised to find that.' Mr Stewart asked, 'Are you going as far as to say this is conclusive?' Inspector Butler indicated no doubt when he replied, 'In my view, due to the characteristics in the teeth, this is conclusive.'

Evidence was then given by other dental experts, who described how plaster casts had been taken from teeth impressions at Glasgow Dental Hospital. Hay's dental record card was produced, showing he required four fillings. Large diagrams of his teeth were used in court to ensure the jury understood the technical aspects of the evidence.

Two policemen who timed a run from the yew tree in the cemetery back to the school said it took one minute 43 seconds.

Detective Superintendent James Weir said that Hay's attitude was 'one of resentment' when he saw him at Rossie School. When he was asked to account for his movements, Hay said he had watched television, had a game of cards and then went up to the dormitory at about 10.15 p.m. Two boys were in the 'dorm' when he went in. Weir told Hay that his statement was in conflict with other statements. Later, when he asked Hay if he had left the school that night, the boy replied, 'No, I never left the school. I can't change my story now, sir.'

The most dramatic evidence in the case came to light on the fifth day of the trial when Dr John Warren Harvey, lecturer in dental surgery at Glasgow University, entered the witness box. He told the court how he had examined the canine teeth of no fewer than 342 junior soldiers two months after the murder. He was trying to ascertain whether any of their teeth compared with the bite marks on the dead girl.

He looked at more than 1,000 canine teeth in the mouths of the soldiers. Only two had pitted eye teeth and none had pits in opposite canine teeth. He spent more than 200 painstaking hours studying the 29 teeth impressions taken. Only the canine teeth of Hay corresponded with the peculiarly-shaped bite marks on the girl's breast.

Using himself as a guinea pig, Dr Harvey demonstrated to the jury various bite marks. By pressing a copper impression of Hay's canine teeth against his finger he produced the peculiar pale-centred mark which was found on the girl's body. Using a small stick he produced from his pocket, he showed the jury the mark left by a solid object. Then, using a ball-point pen, he showed the court the mark left by a hollow-ended object.

Using Hay's upper right canine tooth, he showed that it left a mark on his finger which was pale in the centre and reddened round about.

When asked by the Solicitor-General if he could go any further than saying it was *possible* that Hay's mouth caused the bite marks, Dr Harvey said, 'I find it extremely difficult to conceive that another mouth would have this number of extraordinary characteristics.'

He said there was a broken edge on one tooth and a hook effect where part of a filling was missing. These were remarkable characteristics when taken together. The mark just below the nipple was quite unlike any mark he had ever seen described in forensic literature.

Dr Harvey described how he had been contacted by Inspector Butler while on holiday in Ireland. Returning to Scotland, he was given twenty-nine plaster models of teeth from impressions. They were identified by number only.

He was able to eliminate 24, leaving 5, including, as it was later revealed, the impression of Hay's teeth. A second set of impressions was taken. From these, Dr Harvey was able to exclude another four — leaving only No 11. The small pits he found in the tips of the upper and lower canines were 'quite dramatic and extraordinary.' He had never seen marks made by teeth which left a pale centre. It was something quite unusual.

Re-examining all twenty-nine of the impressions taken, Dr Harvey found one set which answered the problem of the gaps and the abrasions or tears in the skin. The set which made these extraordinary marks was No 11.

It was at this stage that he decided to make perfectly certain by using different materials and techniques to obtain a third, more finely-detailed impression. A warrant to take the final impression of Hay's teeth was subsequently granted.

Under cross-examination, Dr Harvey told the court that 80 per cent of the people in court might have hollows in their teeth but these were completely different from the strange pits in Hay's teeth. Asked if he could exclude the possibility of another mouth in Great Britain making the bite marks, he said he would find it extremely difficult to believe that such a mouth existed.

After more than five hours in the witness

box, the doctor was unshaken in his conviction that the bite marks on Linda Peacock's body were made by Hay.

On the sixth day of the trial, Gordon Hay spent more than two hours in the witness box. Looking perfectly cool, calm and collected, he strongly denied that he was out of the school on the night Linda Peacock was murdered. He did agree, however, that he had left the school a few times to meet girls when he was not supposed to be out. He also agreed that he told lies in several of the statements he made to the police. He denied that his two room-mates were his alibi. The two boys he claimed, were telling lies and Mr Davies, the deputy headmaster, must be mistaken if he said he last saw him at 9.45 p.m. that night. Hay told the court he had been convicted of breaking and entering at Aberdeen Sheriff Court in December 1966 and arrived at Loaningdale Approved School in January 1967. He said he had never been convicted of assault.

He had seen Linda Peacock in Biggar a couple of times but had never spoken to her. The day before she was murdered, he went with two other boys and a master to the pictures in Biggar; that evening, they went to a fair. A girl came across and spoke to one of the boys. He did not know her at the time but he now knew it was Linda Peacock. He did not speak to her at all. Asked if he had said he would not mind going out with Linda, Hay replied, 'Yes.'

Hay said that he remembered another boy producing a metal hook and saying he was going to get someone with it. He told the boy he would only get into trouble and took the hook from him and threw it on top of a cupboard. The next time he saw the hook was in court.

He also denied saying to anyone that he intended going to Biggar, and claimed never to have left the school at all that evening. He had won a prize at a whist drive in the school and, before supper, changed into a white shirt with his pyjama bottoms. He did not think he had a dressing gown on. He was wearing his boots as he did not like the school sandals. After supper, he watched *The Untouchables* on television, which finished at 9.55 p.m. He then went to the dining room to watch a game of cards. At 10.02 p.m. he spoke to another boy and they checked their watches. He spoke to another boy for ten or fifteen minutes, returning to his dormitory between 10.15 and 10.30 p.m. One of his room-mates was already there; the second came in afterwards.

They got into bed and a member of the

staff turned out the lights. Later the boys spoke to the housemother when she arrived back by car and then listened to the radio, which was switched off about midnight. Hay denied having had a conversation the next day with one of the boys about what they would tell the police concerning the murder.

Hay recalled being visited by detectives at Rossie School after he had been transferred there. They greeted him: 'Hello, Gordon. You weren't expecting to see us again, were you?'

They said to him in the presence of the headmaster: 'We know you did it, Gordon. Why not admit it?'

When the detectives went out, Hay was left alone with the headmaster, who told him: 'They know you did it. I know you did it. Why not admit it?'

After being taken to Lanark, he was returned to Rossie, where he told the headmaster, 'My nose was skinned.' The headmaster asked him what had happened and he told him a detective had hit him. He also told the headmaster the police banged his head against a wall a couple of times and put him in a cell. They kept trying to get him to admit it.

Mr Ewan Stewart, cross-examining, said, 'You are just lying to try to blacken everyone?' But Hay denied this.

Hay agreed he had sneaked out of the school and back again without the staff finding out. But he denied he had his eye on Linda. He admitted he had not always told the same story about his movements that night.

During the rigorous cross-examination, Hay remained completely unruffled, putting on an altogether calm and convincing performance. Re-examined by his own counsel, he again denied he was out of the school that night and denied killing Linda.

On the final day of the hearing of evidence, a dental expert called for the defence threw a small spanner in the works when he cast doubt on the significance of the bite marks. Professor George Beagrie, Professor of Restorative Dentistry at Edinburgh University, said he found it difficult to determine what the Crown experts meant by their statements that defects in canine teeth were rare.

He had carried out an experiment with fifty teeth impressions from his own department and found teeth with pits similar to those which the Crown said Hay's teeth showed. He accepted that the bite mark could have been made by Hay but he did not feel it was beyond reasonable doubt. The incidence of defective canine teeth was greater than the Crown experts said. He felt that there could be other mouths in Great Britain that could have caused the bite marks.

Addressing the jury, the Solicitor-General said the case had 'some unusual features'. A certain amount of evidence against Hay was dental and pathological evidence concerning the bite marks. It was clear from the dental evidence, he said, that the only set of teeth out of the twenty-nine that could have made the bite was Hay's.

He said there was no criticism of Linda Peacock of a sexual character. She was not sexually promiscuous. The jury might think it was highly unlikely that she would go voluntarily into the graveyard with some stray tramp who just chanced to meet her on the road. She would only have accompanied someone she knew to that place.

Hay, he said, must have 'worn the cloak of invisibility' for he had not been seen after 9.50 p.m. by six of the masters at his school. His alibi should thus be rejected, root and branch.

When he came to deal with forensic odontology, Mr Stewart said: 'We are not dabbling in some kind of experimental matter. There have been cases on the Continent and in England in which this form of identification has been used. But even supposing there were other people with this kind of mouth existing in the world or even in Britain, how many of these people had on August 5 been expressing a sexual interest in Linda Peacock? How many were living within two minutes of the cemetery? How many were sneaking back into their beds about ten minutes after the murder with their hair blown about and dirt on their faces and clothing? How many had in their possession an instrument such as a hook? How many of these people were next day trying to get their friends to tell lies? There is only one verdict here which an objective and just appraisal and evaluation of the evidence can lead to — a verdict of guilty.'

Mr Ian Stewart, for the defence, said this was the first case of its kind in Scotland in which forensic odontology had been used. In Britain this science was in its infancy. Sixteen characteristics were required in fingerprints but that was not the case here. In Britain, he said, the experience of the dental profession was very limited in this type of case. Only one dentist had said it was beyond reasonable doubt that Hay's teeth caused the bite marks.

The fact that Hay had lied on occasion and may have lied in evidence did not make him the murderer, Mr Stewart argued. If the

Crown broke Hay's alibi that still did not make him the murderer. The evidence for the Crown was circumstantial; the case was balanced 'on a knife edge.' The only evidence that connected Hay with the crime and, moreover, with the scene of the crime, was related to bite marks.

In his two-hour charge to the jury, gravel-voiced Lord Grant warned that circumstantial evidence was not enough to convict Hay. 'For that reason,' he said, 'the dental and pathological evidence is of paramount importance. This forensic odontology, as it is called, is a relatively new science but there must, of course, always be a first time.'

Lord Grant reminded the jury that scientific and medical knowledge advanced as the years went on. It was only comparatively recently that fingerprints had come to be accepted as infallible. It was only in 1945 that palm prints had been recognized. It was of importance that the law should keep pace with science.

Lord Grant said that the case was, as well as a grave one, in some ways unique, difficult and puzzling. But he thought it right to say that he and the jury had been assisted in their task by the way in which it had been prepared and also by the admirable presentation by the

Solicitor-General, Mr Ewan Stewart and his colleague, Mr Ian Stewart, for the defence.

Lord Grant pointed out to the jury that even if Hay had told lies that was not sufficient to establish his guilt. They must therefore examine the evidence on the bite marks with care and in the light of their assessment of the expert witnesses. In assessing the evidence, he continued, the jury should keep in mind that the Crown experts had both made a special study of forensic odontology. The two experts for the defence, on the other hand, were being pushed rather beyond the field where their own expert knowledge lay.

The judge's dismissal of the defence experts' evidence was probably a crucial factor in the jury's deliberations and must have removed any doubts in their minds about the strength and weight of the scientific evidence for the Crown.

After an absence of two and a half hours, the jury returned a majority verdict of Guilty. The judge ordered Hay to be detained during Her Majesty's pleasure as he was under eighteen when he committed the crime.

Hay showed no emotion as he was led away. Sitting in court were his grey-haired mother, Mrs Hannah Hay, and the mother of his victim, Mrs Mary Peacock.

Mrs Hay said afterwards that her husband, Robert, a farm labourer, died on the day after Gordon's sixteenth birthday. 'Up till then, Gordon was fairly happy and content but I think his dad's death had an effect on him. After that, I saw an awful change in my boy. He seemed to go completely off the rails.'

Gordon wrote to his mother twice a week while he was awaiting trial. His mother said: 'I always looked forward to his letters. He's my son and I can forgive him although I can never believe he did this terrible thing. I will stand by him.'

Gordon Hay was a country-born boy who loved cars and often boasted about girl-friends. His love of cars got him into trouble and led to him being sent to an approved school. He danced well and was admired by the girls but friends said he was basically a loner.

Linda's parents, however, could never forget or forgive. Her father said afterwards the school should never have been in Biggar at all and that he would support any move to have it closed down.

Mrs Peacock spoke of her ordeal and her bitterness. 'Linda was a lovely young girl whose life was cut short viciously by a boy from that school,' she said.

It was the third time that tragedy had

struck the Peacock family. Two years earlier, Linda's elder sister died after an illness and a year before that her uncle, a ship's cook, drowned in a dockside accident in England.

Hay's appeal two months later in the Court of Criminal Appeal in Edinburgh was heard by a bench of five judges because of the important legal question of whether the sheriff had the right to issue the warrant to take further teeth impressions from Hay before he was charged.

Lord Clyde, Lord Justice General, presided with Lords Guthrie, Migdale, Cameron and Johnston.

Mr Ian Stewart, in a strong argument, contended that the dental evidence obtained under the warrant was inadmissible and was prejudicial to Hay. The police were not entitled to search the person of a suspect before arrest, he claimed. His argument was particularly concerned with the search of a person as a means of identification rather than to find objects in his possession.

Police powers on identification were limited to such observation as was possible without interfering with the person. Interference with the person without consent and before the individual's arrest was technically an assault. It was a principle of Scottish criminal law that you could not search a person before arresting him.

Mr Stewart argued that there is always a conflict between the rights of an individual and the rights of the state. The right of the state to override the rights of the individual was a matter on which Parliament alone should legislate; it was not for the court to overrule a principle of personal liberty established for many years.

The Solicitor-General argued for the Crown that although the warrant in question was unique there was nothing unlawful about it. If the court could not accept that proposition, the circumstances in the case were such that an irregularity fell to be excused.

Moreover, there was a general power for magistrates to grant warrants for the advancement of the course of justice. In the present case, there had been insufficient evidence to put Hay on trial and the Crown wished to confirm further evidence. The warrant, the Solicitor-General argued, was perfectly valid in the special circumstances. There was no unfairness. Everything was done in the public interest and in the interests of the accused.

The five judges rejected the appeal and on 30 May 1968 gave their reasons. Lord Clyde said that although Hay was not present or legally represented at the hearing for the warrant, the presence of an independent judicial officer, such as the sheriff, afforded the basis for a fair reconciliation of the interests of the public in the suppression of crime and of the individual, who was entitled not to have the liberty of his person or premises unduly jeopardised.

The hearing before the sheriff was by no means a formality; the court had to be satisfied that the circumstances justified the unusual course that had been taken and that the warrant was not too wide or oppressive. The sheriff was the safeguard against the granting of too general a warrant. A warrant of this limited kind would, however, be granted only in special circumstances.

The judge held that the warrant was quite legal and the resulting evidence therefore admissible. Apart from anything else, there was in this case an element of urgency; a visit to the dentist or an injury to Hay's teeth could have destroyed the evidence.

After the conviction, there was a public outcry against the approved school. Biggar Town Council demanded it should be closed immediately or, at least, that the whole staff from the headmaster down should be changed. Provost James Telfer said that since 1963, when Loaningdale opened, the town had wanted a public inquiry into the running of the school. 'We got it during the trial. The security there was terrible,' he said.

In 1965, the Town Council, worried by a spate of petty crimes, demanded a meeting with the school's board of managers. It was an experimental school set up to rehabilitate young boys. A spokesman for the Scottish Education Department said at the time that it was not a penal institution to keep children permanently out of the community. Only boys who were thought capable of returning to society in a matter of months were to be admitted to the school.

Security at Loaningdale was tightened in January 1968, after the council met Mr Bruce Millan, the Under-Secretary of State responsible for education. A night alarm system was installed to alert staff to any break-out. If any boy left the school without permission he was immediately sent to a stricter establishment. But Councillor James Stephen summed up the feelings of local people when he said, 'There is no doubt that this experiment has failed. You cannot cure a bad boy by permissiveness. And when prizes of cigarettes are given out at whist drives and thirteen-year-olds are allowed to smoke, the whole thing is ridiculous.'

The headmaster, who was on holiday at the

time of the murder, was in favour of trying to rehabilitate young offenders. He allowed smoking in the school and allowed the boys to call masters by their Christian names. He recommended Hay's transfer to another school because he did not think he was suitable for Loaningdale.

Provost Telfer, who joined the board of the school in 1965 after the first row, said, 'If it was left to the people of Biggar, it would be closed immediately. There is a tremendous amount of ill-feeling in the town about it. Since the murder, there has been a fantastic amount of complaints by people who have not voiced them before.'

Councillor Stephen, who canvassed more than 20,000 signatures for his petition calling for the return of the death penalty, said the Loaningdale experiment — it was the first 'open' type of school in Scotland — had failed lamentably. The petty dictators of St Andrews House, he said, had decreed it would be sited at Biggar regardless of local feeling.

A spokesman for the Social Work Services Group at the Scottish Office said: 'There have been, and always will be, enormous difficulties in rehabilitating young people who have been out of step with society. It is difficult to talk about success or failure in a social

293

education context.'

At the time, there were 36 boys in Loaningdale: 31 for theft, 3 for truancy and 2 for road traffic offences. This did not suggest the school was harbouring would-be killers.

After the meeting with Mr Millan, two more local people, a doctor and a minister, were added to the board of the school, of which Lord Birsay was chairman.

A Government spokesman summed up the difficulties of rehabilitation when he said: 'Selection is a basic part of the experiment. A boy's record, IQ, family history and condition are all considered. In addition, great weight is given to an assessment of the willingness of a family to co-operate in treatment and of inter-family relationships.'

Linda Peacock's parents at first considered suing the Scottish Education Department, who were responsible for selection of the boys sent to the school. Eventually, however, they accepted £2,000 compensation from the Criminal Injuries Board.

Mrs Peacock said:

The money is no compensation for Linda's life. We are more interested in punishment for all those responsible for the negligent system that led to her death. We had considered a civil action but have now dropped that as the only measure a civil court might take would be to award damages, which is little comfort to us.

Writing in the Glasgow Police magazine some time later, Dr Warren Harvey, in an article called 'The Tooth, the Whole Truth and the Police' revealed that twenty-five dentists were now linked with the police in Aberdeen, Dundee, Edinburgh and Glasgow to help in criminal cases. When a victim is bitten, Harvey wrote, the marks must be seen at the first possible moment by a dentist, a police photographer and a pathologist. He pointed out that the Biggar murder trial verdict was by a majority of 14 to 1 and that about one third of the 1,100 foolscap pages in the transcript of the evidence consisted of dental and medical evidence.

But, a few years later, allegations by an internationally known expert on forensic odontology, Dr Soren Keiser-Nielsen of the Department of Forensic Odontology at the Royal Dental College in Copenhagen, cast a slight shadow over the new science. He alleged that he came to Scotland before the trial but his evidence had been 'hushed up' and he had been hurriedly got out of the way. In a letter to the Forensic Society's journal, he said he concluded there was nothing in the mark on the victim's breast to indicate it was a bite mark. Even if it were, he added, there were too few points of similarity to warrant a dental identification of the originator. He had explained his reasoning and conclusions, and asked whether the fact he had drawn conclusions adverse to the Crown case would come to the notice of the defence.

But the Crown revealed that the doctor had considered the evidence insufficient to justify a firm conclusion on identification and had declined to give evidence. Counsel for the defence had accordingly been informed by the Crown that Dr Keiser-Neilsen was not willing to give evidence.

The Crown also said the doctor's views expressed at the time did not match the views he expressed later. He had undoubtedly withdrawn, declining to give evidence. Mr Alistair R. Brownlie, Secretary of the Society of Solicitors in the Supreme Courts of Scotland, strongly denied the doctor's allegations. The doctor, Mr Brownlie maintained, had indicated he wanted nothing more to do with the case and was therefore not called as a witness. The police who drove him to the airport were merely exercising the customary courtesies. The doctor was not, as he later claimed, hurriedly got out of the way.

But the controversy still did not die down. Keiser-Nielsen insisted in 1972 that the mark on Linda Peacock's breast was not a human bite mark. Hay's counsel, Mr Ian Stewart, recalled being told the doctor was not prepared to come and give evidence and that there was no point in calling him as a witness if he was unwilling to come.

While there is little likelihood of compulsory dental examination becoming a standard feature of Scottish pre-trial criminal procedure, the courts clearly recognised the exceptional nature of the case in approving the warrant to take the vital third impression of Hay's teeth. The power given to the prosecution to secure that important evidence from the previously inviolable person of the suspect might well be used again if the course of justice demands it.

Had genetic fingerprinting, which has been hailed as the greatest breakthrough in forensic science this century, been available at that time, even more conclusive proof might well have been provided by the scientists.

We do hope that you have enjoyed reading this large print book.

Did you know that all of our titles are available for purchase?

We publish a wide range of high quality large print books including:
**Romances, Mysteries, Classics
General Fiction
Non Fiction and Westerns**

Special interest titles available in large print are:
**The Little Oxford Dictionary
Music Book
Song Book
Hymn Book
Service Book**

Also available from us courtesy of Oxford University Press:
**Young Readers' Dictionary
(large print edition)
Young Readers' Thesaurus
(large print edition)**

For further information or a free brochure, please contact us at:
**Ulverscroft Large Print Books Ltd.,
The Green, Bradgate Road, Anstey,
Leicester, LE7 7FU, England.
Tel:** (00 44) 0116 236 4325
Fax: (00 44) 0116 234 0205

Other titles in the
Ulverscroft Large Print Series:

PLAIN DEALER

William Ardin

Antique dealing has its own equivalent to 'insider trading', as Charles Ramsay finds out to his cost. Offered the purchase of a lifetime, he sees all his ambitions realised in an antique jade cup, known as the 'Loot'. But as soon as the deal is irrevocably struck he finds himself stuck with it like an albatross around his neck — unable to export it without a licence, unable to sell it at home, and in a paralysing no man's land where nobody has sufficient capital to take it off his hands . . .

NO TIME LIKE THE PRESENT

June Barraclough

Daphne Berridge, who has never married, has retired to the small Yorkshire village of Heckcliff where she grew up, intending to write the biography of an eighteenth-century woman poet. Two younger women are interested in her project: Cressida, Daphne's niece, who lives in London, and is uncertain about the direction of her life; and Judith, who keeps a shop in Heckcliff, and is a divorcee. When an old friend of Daphne falls in love with Judith, the question — as for Cressida — is marriage or independence. Then Daphne also receives a surprise proposal.

SEARCH FOR A SHADOW

Kay Christopher

On the last day of her holiday Rosemary Roberts met an intriguing American in the foyer of her London hotel. By some extraordinary coincidence, Larry Madison-Jones was due to visit the tiny Welsh village where Rosemary lived. But how much of a coincidence was Larry's erratic presence there? The moment Rosemary returned home, her life took on a subtle, though sinister edge — Larry had a secret he was not willing to share. As Rosemary was drawn deeper into a web of mysterious and suspicious occurrences, she found herself wondering if Larry really loved her — or was trying to drive her mad . . .

THREE WISHES

Barbara Delinsky

Slipping and sliding in the snow as she walks home from the restaurant where she's worked for fourteen years, Bree Miller barely has time to notice the out-of-control lorry, headed straight for her. All Bree remembers of that fateful night is a bright light, and a voice granting her three wishes. Are they real or imagined? And who is the man standing over her bedside when finally she wakes up? Soon Bree finds herself the recipient of precisely those things she'd most wanted in life — even that which had seemed beyond all reasonable hope.

WEB OF WAR

Hilary Grenville

Claire Grant, a radar operator in the WAAF, still mourning the death of her parents and brother in an air raid, finds coming on leave to her grandmother's home difficult to face. Martin, a friend from her school days, now a pilot in the RAF, helps her to come to terms with her grief and encourages the flimsy rapport between Claire and her grandmother. War rules their lives and it is some time before they meet again. Claire is in love, but there are many quirks of fate yet to be faced.

SUSAN IN AMERICA

Jane Aiken Hodge

Susan has high hopes of her American trip. Shy and studious at Oxford, she felt herself always on the outside of things there. Surely everything will be different at Radcliffe College, where she has a year's fellowship. But in New England she is lonelier than ever. Her tutorials with glamorous Professor Winter soon become the high points of her week, but when their intellectual cut and thrust leads on to passion, she finds herself in uncharted waters, risking shipwreck among the strict conventions of 1930s Boston society.